Discovering Jesus in Exodus

D1716579

Susan Hunt & Richie Hunt

CROSSWAY BOOKS • WHEATON, ILLINOIS

A DIVISION OF GOOD NEWS PUBLISHERS

Discovering Jesus in Exodus
Copyright © 2004 by Susan Hunt and Richie Hunt
Published by Crossway Books
a division of Good News Publishers
1300 Crescent Street
Wheaton, Illinois 60187

All rights reserved. No part of this publication may be reproduced,
stored in a retrieval system, or transmitted in any form by any means, electronic,
mechanical, photocopy, recording, or otherwise, without the prior permission
of the publisher, except as provided by USA copyright law.

Cover design: Cindy Kiple
Cover illustration: Nancy Munger
First printing 2004
Printed in the United States of America

Scripture is taken from the Holy Bible: English Standard Version.
Copyright © 2001 by Good News Publishers. Used by permission. All rights reserved.

Scripture designated NIV is taken from the Holy Bible: New International Version®. Copyright © 1973, 1978, 1984
by International Bible Society. Used by permission of Zondervan Publishing House. All rights reserved.
The "NIV" and "New International Version" trademarks are registered in the United States Patent and Trademark Office
by International Bible Society. Use of either trademark requires the permission of International Bible Society.

Scripture references marked NKJV are taken from the New King James Version.
Copyright © 1982, Thomas Nelson, Inc. Used by permission.

Library of Congress Cataloging-in-Publication Data

Hunt, Susan, 1940-
  Discovering Jesus in Exodus / Susan Hunt & Richie Hunt.
    p. cm. -- (Covenant promises for covenant kids)
  Summary: Pastor Scotty uses stories, sports, and Bible study to teach
the children at Covenant Kids Club about Jesus and the covenant
between God and man.
  ISBN 1-58134-453-8 (tpb)
  [1. Clergy--Fiction. 2. Clubs--Fiction. 3. Christian life—Fiction. 4.
God—Promises. 5. Jesus Christ.] I. Hunt, Richie, 1967- II. Title.
PZ7.H916534Di 2004
[Fic]--dc22
                2003027533

CH   14   13   12   11   10   09   08   07   06   05   04
15   14   13   12   11   10   9   8   7   6   5   4   3   2   1

CROSSWAY BOOKS BY SUSAN HUNT AND RICHIE HUNT

Big Truths for Little Kids

Discovering Jesus in Genesis

Discovering Jesus in Exodus

CROSSWAY BOOKS BY SUSAN HUNT

By Design

My ABC Bible Verses

Spiritual Mothering

The True Woman

Heirs of the Covenant

Your Home—a Place of Grace

CROSSWAY BOOKS BY SUSAN HUNT AND BARBARA THOMPSON

The Legacy of Biblical Womanhood

DEDICATION

To the newest members of our clan:

Maggie Grace Coley

Heather Joy Hunt

And to their older cousins:

Hunter, Mary Kate, Daniel, Susie, Sam, Mac, Angus, Cassie, and Scotty

And to the covenant children of Midway Presbyterian Church (PCA):

These stories are about you and for you.

Thank you for giving us ideas and inspiration.

Contents

Dear Parents:

This series is our effort to put the concepts from *Heirs of the Covenant* and *Your Home—A Place of Grace* into stories for families. We want children to have the glorious experience of discovering Jesus on every page of Scripture. We want them to see what the disciples saw:

> That very day two of them were going to a village named Emmaus. . . . While they were talking and discussing together, Jesus himself drew near and went with them. But their eyes were kept from recognizing him. And he said to them, "What is this conversation that you are holding with each other as you walk?" And they stood still, looking sad. . . .
>
> And he said to them, "O foolish ones, and slow of heart to believe all that the prophets have spoken! Was it not necessary that the Christ should suffer these things and enter into his glory?"
>
> **And beginning with Moses and all the Prophets, he interpreted to them in all the Scriptures the things concerning himself.** . . . And their eyes were opened and they recognized him. And he vanished from their sight.
>
> They said to each other, "Did not our hearts burn within us while he talked to us on the road, while he opened to us the Scriptures?"
>
> And they rose that same hour and returned to Jerusalem. And they found the eleven and those who were with them gathered together, saying, "The Lord has risen indeed. . . ." (Luke 24:13ff.)

When our children see Jesus in all of Scripture, they will begin to see the covenantal framework of Scripture and of life. A covenant is a binding agreement. God bound Himself to His people in a covenant of grace. His relationship with His people is to be mirrored in their relationships with one another. The covenant is a way of life that flows out of a promise of life. A covenantal perspective will give our children the foundation for a robust faith and life. This comprehensive worldview will give them a passion to find others and proclaim, "The Lord has risen indeed!"

Our Prayer for This Book

Exodus confronts us with an emerging picture of the church. Adoption is a dominant theme. At Sinai God adopted Israel as His people. The church is the spiritual Israel.

Our prayer is that a biblical understanding of adoption will help shape our children's perspective of their identity in Christ. Whether your children are biological or adopted, our passion is for them to know that when God adopts us, we belong to Him and to one another.

Exodus challenges us to assume our privileges and responsibilities as a part of God's covenant family. The concept of covenant life is diminished in a culture of individualism where mutual good is sacrificed for personal pleasure.

Our prayer is that this book will awaken in children a transcendent wonder of the privilege of being a part of the church of the living God, an awareness of the responsibility of this privilege, and a deep and abiding love for God's church. We pray that families will learn how to live in covenant with God and with one another.

How to Use This Book

We use these stories with children ages four to twelve. As younger children hear the stories, they begin to learn the language and ways of covenant life. Older children begin to comprehend a covenantal perspective of faith and life and to see how God's truth is integrated into all of life. The following questions guide us as we write, and we hope they will help you and your children think biblically and live covenantally. We pray that they will help you to discover Jesus in all of Scripture:

• What covenant promise do we see in this story?

• What do we learn about Jesus?

• What is our privilege and responsibility because of God's promise and His character?

Involve your children in the story. Let them answer questions and read the Bible verses.

Use the questions at the end of each story, but also engage your child in additional conversations to make application to his or her life.

We encourage you to memorize the Scripture verses with your children. If your children are younger, you may want to select one or two verses to memorize. Scripture memorization plants God's Word in their minds, and we can trust the Holy Spirit to use that Word to teach, convict, and convince them all through life.

> *"For the mountains may depart and the hills be removed,*
> *but my steadfast love shall not depart from you,*
> *and my covenant of peace shall not be removed,"*
> *says the LORD, who has compassion on you. . . .*
> *"All your children shall be taught by the LORD,*
> *And great shall be the peace of your children."*
> ISAIAH 54:10, 13

CHARACTERS

(These characters were introduced in *Big Truths for Little Kids* and *Discovering Jesus in Genesis*.)

Cassie and Caleb: This brother and sister are the primary characters in *Big Truths for Little Kids* and *Discovering Jesus in Genesis*.

Pop and Mimi: Cassie and Caleb's grandparents.

Sir John: An elderly gentleman who moved from Scotland to live with his daughter.

Miss Jenny: Sir John's daughter. She lives on the same street with Cassie and Caleb.

Granny Grace: This widow lives across the street from Cassie and Caleb.

Mary and Mac: Granny Grace's grandchildren. They came with their mom to live with Granny Grace when their dad left the family.

Daniel: He lives next door to Cassie and Caleb.

Hunter: The youth pastor at the church.

Pastor Scotty: The pastor of the church.

Angus and Susie: Pastor Scotty's children.

— ■ —

NEW CHARACTERS IN THIS BOOK

Heather: Pastor Scotty's wife.

Papa Sam and Mama Maggie: Pastor Scotty's parents.

Grace and Joy: Twins adopted by Pastor Scotty's family.

Shannon: Cassie and Caleb's older cousin.

James, Jason, Kellie, and Laurin: Cassie and Caleb's cousins.

Uncle Dean and Aunt Kathryn: Cassie and Caleb's uncle and aunt.

PART 1

THE COVENANT PROMISE

Jesus Christ

Part 1 forms the foundation for the rest of the book. In this section the children are introduced to Ephesians 1:3-7. This passage provides a schematic to understand all of Scripture. The concepts that are introduced in Part 1 are expanded throughout the book.

> *Praise be to the God and Father of our Lord Jesus Christ, who has blessed us in the heavenly realms with every spiritual blessing in Christ. For he chose us in him before the creation of the world to be holy and blameless in his sight. In love he predestined us to be adopted as his sons through Jesus Christ, in accordance with his pleasure and will—to the praise of his glorious grace, which he has freely given us in the One he loves. In him we have redemption through his blood. . . . (Ephesians 1:3-7 NIV)*

CHAPTER ONE

Chosen

For he chose us in him before the creation of the world. . . . (Ephesians 1:4 niv)

———■———

Pastor Scotty sat at his desk reading his Bible. "I sure get excited about teaching God's Word to our covenant children," he said out loud. Then he laughed at himself for talking out loud when no one was there. He prayed, "Father, thank You for allowing me to teach Your children about Your grace. Please give the kids hearts to know You and to love You. In Jesus' name, amen."

He jumped up, grabbed his whistle, and bolted out the door. "Time to go!" he shouted as he hurried down the hall.

Pastor Scotty had been a football player in college. He was a pretty tough guy, but he had a big, tender heart that almost exploded with love for the kids in his church. One of his favorite things was playing with and teaching the children at Covenant Kids Club.

The kids were already gathering on the playground. "What're we going to play?" they called as Pastor Scotty approached them.

"I've got a great game," he answered, "but I need to choose a team. I choose Cassie, Caleb, Daniel, Mary, Mac . . ." On and on he went until he had chosen every child except Angus and Susie.

"Well, now I have my team," he announced.

Angus and Susie knew that he was teasing them. Pastor Scotty looked at them and asked, "Who are you? Have I seen you before?" All the kids laughed.

"Dad, you're so funny," grinned Susie.

Angus just shook his head. "Well, he tries to be funny."

"Come on. I guess I'll choose you." Pastor Scotty chuckled.

Susie and Angus thought it was cool being the preacher's kids, and they loved the way their dad teased them.

"Well, now that that's settled. What're we going to play?" asked Caleb.

"Play? Oh, I hadn't thought about a game. I just wanted to choose all of you because I love you so much," joked Pastor Scotty. Then he divided them into two teams for a game of kickball.

When the game was over, everyone went inside for refreshments. "Hi, Miss Heather," the kids called as Pastor Scotty's wife greeted them.

"Give me a hug, and I'll give you some cookies," she said. The kids loved Miss Heather. She was as short as Pastor Scotty was tall.

When the children finished eating, they settled down for the lesson.

Pastor Scotty blew his whistle and said, "Let's play football. It's you against me! I'm big and you're little, but if you think hard, you can beat me. The ball is on the twenty-yard line. Each time you answer a question correctly, you move your ball five yards. First question: If you are going to tell a story, where should you begin?"

"At the beginning," the children responded.

"Nope!" said Pastor Scotty triumphantly. "Not this time. We're going to start *before* the beginning. Turn to Ephesians 1:3-7."

Pages turned and Pastor Scotty read:

"'*Praise be to the God and Father of our Lord Jesus Christ, who has blessed us in the heavenly realms with every spiritual blessing in Christ. For he chose us in him before the creation of the world to be holy and blameless in his sight. In love he predestined us to be adopted as his sons through Jesus Christ, in accordance with his pleasure and will—to the praise of his glorious grace, which he has freely given us in the One he loves. In him we have redemption through his blood. . . .*'" (NIV)

"Pastor Scotty," exclaimed Mary, "that reminds me of what you did! You chose all of us to be on your team."

Pastor Scotty's whole face lit up in a grin as he shouted, "Go, Mary! You just moved the ball five yards. Now you're on the fifteen-yard line. Let's keep this drive going. *When* did God choose us?"

Everyone read the passage to find the answer. Daniel found it first and called, "Before the creation of the world."

"See—I told you we were going to start before the beginning. Now we're on the ten-yard line," roared Pastor Scotty. "*Why* did God choose us to belong to Him? Is it because we are so smart or good or cute? You'll find the answer in Deuteronomy 7:6-8."

Pages turned as the kids tried to find the answer. Mac stood up. "I've got it. It's because He loves us."

Everyone clapped and yelled, "Five-yard line!"

"You're almost ready to score, but let's take a time-out. Mac, read the verses for us."

Mac read:

> "'*For you are a people holy to the LORD your God. The LORD your God has chosen you to be a people for his treasured possession, out of all the peoples who are on the face of the earth. It was not because you were more in number than any other people that the LORD set his love on you . . . but it is because the LORD loves you. . . .'*" (Deuteronomy 7:6-8)

"Pastor Scotty," said Mary, "that reminds me of you too. You chose all of us to be on your team because you love us so much."

Pastor Scotty threw his hands up in the air and shouted, "Touchdown!" so loudly the kids almost jumped out of their seats. Then he started doing his silly victory dance while the kids chanted, "Go, Pastor Scotty. Go, Pastor Scotty."

Finally everyone calmed down. Pastor Scotty got a serious look on his face, and the kids knew that he was going to tell them something very important. They listened carefully. "I do love you, kids, but my love does not compare to God's love for us. Before the world was created, God the Father, Son, and Holy Spirit made a covenant, or an agreement, to redeem the people He chose in Christ to be His own. The glorious Creator God chose us in Christ, and He bound Himself to us in covenant love. Now that's big."

———■———

LET'S TALK

Who are Pastor Scotty's children?

What is Pastor Scotty's wife's name?

What did God do before He created the world?

Why did God choose us?

CHAPTER TWO

Holy and Blameless

For he chose us . . . to be holy and blameless in his sight. (Ephesians 1:4)

"I wonder what Pastor Scotty has planned," mused Caleb as they drove to the church for Covenant Kids Club.

"And why does he want our dads to come?" asked Cassie.

"Maybe you're all in trouble, and he wants to tell your dads how bad you've been," teased their dad as he parked the car.

"I don't think so," laughed Caleb. "I'm sure that whatever he has planned is wild and crazy."

"What makes you think that?" quizzed his dad.

"Well, those towels you brought are a pretty good clue," Caleb replied.

They climbed out of the car and ran to join the others who had gathered around Pastor Scotty and Hunter, the youth pastor. Pastor Scotty blew his whistle, and everyone got quiet. "We've got a great game," he announced. "Kids, you're going inside with Hunter, and your dads are going to hide. Then you have to find an adult and tag him. Let's go!"

The kids followed Hunter. After a few minutes he brought them back outside, counted to three, and they were off. "This is easy," Mac shouted. "They're all lined up over there behind those bushes. Come on—let's go tag them."

Pastor Scotty whispered to the dads, "Stay down, men. Don't shoot until I tell you. We'll wait until we see the whites of their eyes!"

The kids were running and yelling, "We see you! You can't hide from us!"

The men stayed perfectly still until Pastor Scotty shouted, "Fire!"

Suddenly they stood up and blasted the kids with super-soaker water guns. The kids were so startled they didn't move for several seconds. By this time they were drenched. Then the kids remembered their weapons. Hunter had given each of them a can of shaving cream. Now the dripping-wet kids charged the dads and covered them with foamy white stuff!

Pastor Scotty and Hunter were laughing so hard they almost lost their breath. Finally Pastor Scotty blew his whistle and shouted, "Truce!"

Dads and kids were a soggy mess. They wrapped up in towels, and everyone sat on the ground for the lesson.

"Let's say the memory verses we're learning," began Pastor Scotty. The kids recited:

> *"'Praise be to the God and Father of our Lord Jesus Christ, who has blessed us in the heavenly realms with every spiritual blessing in Christ. For he chose us in him before the creation of the world to be holy and blameless in his sight. In love he predestined us to be adopted as his sons through Jesus Christ, in accordance with his pleasure and will—to the praise of his glorious grace, which he has freely given us in the One he loves. In him we have redemption through his blood. . . .'" (Ephesians 1:3-7* NIV)

"When did God choose us?" asked Pastor Scotty.

"Before the creation of the world," answered the kids.

"What did God choose us to be?" asked Pastor Scotty.

They all said the verses over in their minds to find the answer. Angus called out, "Holy and blameless in His sight."

"Touchdown!" yelled Pastor Scotty. He opened his Bible and read, "'Christ loved the church and gave himself up for her to make her holy . . . and to present her to himself as a radiant church, without stain or wrinkle or any other blemish, but holy and blameless'" (Ephesians 5:25-27 NIV).

He closed his Bible and asked, "Does this mean that Jesus loves this church building and wants the building to be holy and blameless?"

"I don't think so," answered Daniel. "We learned in Sunday school that the church is God's people."

"Touchdown!" yelled Pastor Scotty. Then he grinned. "Well, does this mean that God does not want us to have stains or wrinkles? You kids look pretty wet and wrinkled to me."

"And our dads are stained with shaving cream," added Caleb.

"I think it means that He wants us to be cleansed from sin," said Mary.

Pastor Scotty didn't yell "touchdown" this time. He had the serious look on his face. The kids listened carefully. "You're exactly right, Mary," he said tenderly. "God is holy, and so there can be no sin in His presence. Jesus lived a holy and blameless life. He never sinned. Then He died in our place, and God put our sin on Him. When we trust Him for forgiveness, God declares that we are holy and blameless in His sight because of what Jesus did for us. Now that's big!"

---■---

LET'S TALK

When did God choose us in Christ to belong to Him?

Why did God choose us to belong to Him?

What did He choose us to be?

CHAPTER THREE

Adopted

He predestined us to be adopted as his sons through Jesus Christ. (Ephesians 1:5)

■

"I can't wait to tell everybody at Covenant Kids Club the good news," said Angus as they drove to the church. "I'm so excited I'm 'bout to bust!"

"Me too," Susie chimed in. "This is great. Everyone is going to be so happy. When can we tell them, Dad?" Susie tended to chatter when she was excited. She didn't even stop for her dad to answer. "There's Cassie and Mary. Can I tell them now, Dad?"

Pastor Scotty and Heather laughed. "Calm down, Susie. We'll wait and tell everyone at the same time when we go inside for our lesson."

"Oh no! I don't know if I can wait. I'm about to pop. I don't even know what I'm saying," babbled Susie.

Susie and Angus loved playing games, but that day they could hardly wait for the play time to be over so they could tell their friends the news. Finally they went inside.

Pastor Scotty blew his whistle. "Our family has some great news to share with you."

Susie and Angus stood up. They had already decided that Susie would talk first. They knew she would get excited and chatter and forget the details. The more orderly Angus would fill in the information she left out.

Susie announced, "This is sooo exciting! It's the greatest thing! You're going to love our news."

Daniel blurted, "What news?"

Susie took a deep breath and spoke in a slow, dramatic voice. "Mom and Dad are going to China to get a baby girl!"

For a few seconds everyone was speechless. Then Cassie asked, "Why are they going to China to get a baby?"

Angus was ready. He had given this a lot of thought. "There are a lot of baby girls in orphanages in China. We've been praying about this for a long time. We believe the Lord wants us to adopt one of these little girls."

"You're going to get a baby sister!" exclaimed Cassie. "That's exciting news."

"And she'll come all the way from China," added Mac.

"When will you get her?" asked Daniel.

Pastor Scotty smiled. "We don't know. But we wanted to tell you so that you can pray for us and for the little girl that the Lord has for us. Now let's recite our memory verses and see if you hear a word that we've been talking about."

The kids recited:

> "'Praise be to the God and Father of our Lord Jesus Christ, who has blessed us in the heavenly realms with every spiritual blessing in Christ. For he chose us in him before the creation of the world to be holy and blameless in his sight. In love he predestined us to be adopted as his sons through Jesus Christ, in accordance with his pleasure and will—to the praise of his glorious grace, which he has freely given us in the One he loves. In him we have redemption through his blood. . . .'" (Ephesians 1:3-7 NIV)

"I know," cried Daniel. "It's *adopted*. God adopts us just like your family is going to adopt a baby from China."

The kids knew what was coming; so they all covered their ears with their hands as Pastor Scotty shouted, "Touchdown!" Then he continued, "When we adopt this baby girl, she'll have a new family and a new home and a new name. When God adopts us, we have a new family—the covenant family. All Christians everywhere in the world, and all Christians who have ever lived, are our brothers and sisters. And we get a new home. Where do you think our new home is?"

"I know," squealed Cassie. "Heaven is our home. But what's our new name, Pastor Scotty?"

"Our new name is Christian," he answered. "Because of our sin we are not born into God's family. Our sin separates us from God. Jesus died to pay for our sin. He gives us His righteousness, and God declares us to be holy and blameless in His sight. God adopts us as His children because He chose us in Christ before He created the world and because Jesus died in our place. We bear Christ's name just like our new daughter will bear our name. Now that's big!"

———◼———

LET'S TALK

What was the exciting news Angus and Susie had?

When God adopts us, who is our family?

When God adopts us, what is our name?

When God adopts us, where is our home?

CHAPTER FOUR

Redeemed

In him we have redemption through his blood. . . . (Ephesians 1:7)

■

"Buckle up and hunker down," instructed Pastor Scotty as his family piled into the car. "I know we have serious shopping to do when we get to the mall, but let's use our driving time well. Kids, say our Covenant Kids' Club memory verses for your mom."

Two voices from the backseat recited together:

> "'Praise be to the God and Father of our Lord Jesus Christ, who has blessed us in the heavenly realms with every spiritual blessing in Christ. For he chose us in him before the creation of the world to be holy and blameless in his sight. In love he predestined us to be adopted as his sons through Jesus Christ, in accordance with his pleasure and will—to the praise of his glorious grace, which he has freely given us in the One he loves. In him we have redemption through his blood. . . .'" (Ephesians 1:3-7 NIV)

"Touchdown!" exclaimed Pastor Scotty.

"Just a minute!" laughed their mom. "They don't score until I say they've scored. I want to know if they understand what they said."

"You can't stump my kids," grinned Pastor Scotty.

"We'll see," teased Heather. "When did God choose us to belong to Him?"

"Before the creation of the world," shouted Angus and Susie.

"Why did God choose us to belong to Him?"

"Because He loves us," answered Angus and Susie.

"Umm, that's pretty good. Here's a harder question. What did God choose you to be?"

"Holy and blameless," came the answer from the backseat.

"Okay, I'll admit that I'm having trouble stumping these covenant kids, but I don't think they can answer this question. How can people who are stained with sin become spotless and blameless before God?"

Angus, the thinker, had been thinking about this a lot; so he was ready. "When Jesus died on the cross, our sin was put on Him. When we trust Him, His righteousness is put on us. God forgives us, and He sees us covered with the righteousness of Jesus."

"Touchdown!" yelled Pastor Scotty. The kids cheered.

Their mom pretended to be baffled. "Where did you people learn all of this?"

"They have a good teacher," quipped Pastor Scotty. "Watch this. Kids, when God forgives us, what does He do for us?"

"He adopts us!" answered the backseat chorus.

"I have one more question, and I'm sure you can't answer this one," said Heather. "What do we have through the blood of Jesus?"

There was silence from the backseat as Angus and Susie slowly recited the verses to find the answer. Both of them shouted at the same time, "Redemption!"

"Those are *my* kids!" Pastor Scotty said to Heather.

"Do you think they need a mom? I'd like to apply for the job," she responded.

Susie giggled. Then she said, "I have a question. What does redemption mean?"

"I'm glad you asked," their dad replied. "To redeem means to buy something back that already belongs to you. We belong to God because He made us, but we're lost in sin. Jesus paid for our sin with His own life. He bought us back. Would you like to hear a story about when I was a kid?"

"Sure," cried the two in the backseat.

"When I was a little boy, I had a baseball that I loved. It was the first ball that I ever bought with my own money. One time when my dad took me to a professional baseball game, one of the players even autographed my baseball. I loved that ball, and I wanted to take it with me everywhere I went. Mom warned me that I was going to lose it, but I was sure I wouldn't. Well, as I hope you have learned, moms are usually right. One day Mom had lots of places to go, and somewhere along the way I lost my baseball. We went back to several stores, but we could

not find my ball. Six months later Dad and I went to a yard sale. There was a table with toys, and what do you think was on that table?"

"Your baseball!"

"Yes! I picked it up, and when I saw the autograph, I knew that it was mine. I was so excited I could hardly breathe. I grabbed it and ran to Dad screaming, 'I found it! I found my baseball!' Dad was as excited as I was. I wanted to hurry home and show Mom, but Dad explained that I couldn't just take the ball. I would have to pay for it. 'But it's mine,' I protested. Dad explained that it belonged to someone else now. 'Then I'll buy it back,' I said as I dug in my pocket and pulled out some money that I had earned pulling weeds from Mom's flowerbed. All the way home I held my baseball. And I still have that old ball. It reminds me that I belonged to God, but I was lost in sin. Then Jesus bought me back. He redeemed me."

"Touchdown!" said their mom softly as she smiled lovingly at Pastor Scotty.

Angus covered his eyes. "Oh no—not those goofy looks."

◼

LET'S TALK

When did God choose us to belong to Him?

Why did God choose us to belong to Him?

What do we have through the blood of Jesus?

What does redeem mean?

What happened to Pastor Scotty's baseball?

PART 2

GLORY STORIES FROM EXODUS

Part 2 includes eight "glory stories" from Exodus. Each Bible story is followed by three application stories designed to help children respond to God's promises in obedience. The covenant privileges and responsibilities that are discussed are trust, humility, worship, thankfulness, love, goodness, mercy, and unity.

Genesis tells the story of God giving the covenant promise to Abraham. The book concludes with Abraham's family going to Egypt. Exodus begins four hundred years later. In faithfulness to His promise to Abraham, the covenant-keeping God had caused Abraham's family to grow into a multitude of families. Exodus is the glorious story of God redeeming His people out of slavery so that they could worship Him. This book is a thrilling picture of the redemption and adoption of those chosen in Christ before the creation of the world.

Exodus presents a stunning picture of the church as God's "chosen people, a royal priesthood, a holy nation, a people belonging to God, that you may declare the praises of him who called you out of darkness into his wonderful light. Once you were not a people, but now you are the people of God; once you had not received mercy, but now you have received mercy" (1 Peter 2:9-10 NIV).

I will take you to be my people, and I will be your God, and you shall know that I am the LORD *your God, who has brought you out from under the burdens of the Egyptians. (Exodus 6:7)*

My presence will go with you, and I will give you rest. (Exodus 33:14)

The LORD*, the* LORD*, a God merciful and gracious, slow to anger, and abounding in steadfast love and faithfulness, keeping steadfast love for thousands, forgiving iniquity and transgression and sin. (Exodus 34:6-7)*

CHAPTER FIVE

Glory Story—God Keeps His Promises

EXODUS 1—2

■

A COVENANT PROMISE:

Now the Lord said to Abram, ". . . I will make of you a great nation, and I will bless you and make your name great, so that you will be a blessing. . . . Know for certain that your offspring will be sojourners in a land that is not theirs and will be servants there, and they will be afflicted for four hundred years. But I will bring judgment on the nation that they serve, and afterward they shall come out with great possessions." (Genesis 12:2; 15:13-14)

A COVENANT PRIVILEGE AND RESPONSIBILITY: TRUST

Some trust in chariots and some in horses, but we trust in the name of the Lord our God. (Psalm 20:7 NIV)

Pastor Scotty looked at the kids sitting in front of him. "Covenant kids, you are part of God's covenant family, and I want you to know your family history. Our history is not about dead people. It's about how God makes His people holy and blameless so that we can live in His presence. The people we talk about are living in His presence right now! Their bodies have died, but their souls are with Jesus! And when we go to heaven, we'll be able to talk to them."

"I can't wait," declared Caleb.

Pastor Scotty laughed. "Before the world was created, God the Father, Son, and Holy Spirit made a covenant to save the people who belonged to Him. When God created Adam and Eve, He made them holy. They reflected His glory. But they disobeyed God. When Adam and

Eve sinned, God promised to send a Savior who would take their punishment so they could live in His presence and reflect His glory again."

"This is a glory story," Cassie announced. "I love glory stories."

Pastor Scotty smiled. "I do too, Cassie. All of the stories in the Bible are glory stories because they tell us about our glorious God. He gave the covenant promise to Adam and Eve, and then many years later He promised Abraham that the Savior would come from his family. God told Abraham that his family would be slaves in Egypt, but He promised that after four hundred years He would redeem them. During the years that the Israelites were in Egypt, they had children, and more children, and more children. Pharaoh was worried about the growing number of Israelites. He thought up a wicked plan. He commanded the Israelite midwives to kill all the baby boys who were born."

"Dad, what's a midwife?" asked Susie.

"Good question. A midwife is like a nurse who helps women when they have babies. God had promised that the Savior would come from Abraham's family. If all the baby boys were killed, the family would end."

"What did the midwives do?" asked Cassie softly.

"Look at your Bibles," instructed Pastor Scotty. "Angus, read verse 17."

Angus read: "'The midwives . . . feared God and did not do what the king of Egypt had told them to do; they let the boys live'" (Exodus 1:17 NIV). Angus looked at his dad. "Wasn't it dangerous for them to disobey Pharaoh?" he asked.

"It certainly was," answered Pastor Scotty. "Why do you think they did this? Look at the verse again."

"I think I see it," squealed Cassie. "They feared God. Umm, so they were afraid of God?"

Pastor Scotty smiled. "Not exactly. This means that they honored, trusted, and obeyed God. They believed He could and would keep His promise to deliver them out of Egypt and to send a Savior. They obeyed God even though it was dangerous."

"What happened to them?" asked Mary.

"Good question," replied Pastor Scotty. "Read verses 20-21."

Mary read: "'So God was kind to the midwives and the people increased and became even more numerous. And because the midwives feared God, he gave them families of their own'" (Exodus 1:20-21 NIV).

Mac was intrigued. "Let me see if I've got this right. Pharaoh tried to get the midwives to kill the Israelite baby boys, and they wouldn't do it; so God gave the midwives babies. Now there were even more Israelites for Pharaoh to worry about."

"You're exactly right!" exclaimed Pastor Scotty. "Pharaoh was furious! He told the Egyptians that when an Israelite baby boy was born, they were to throw him in the Nile River! There were other Israelites who trusted God. A man named Amram and his wife, Jocebed, had a little boy named Aaron and a young daughter named Miriam. Then God gave them another baby—and it was a boy. They hid the baby as long as they could, but he got bigger and cried louder. His mother put him in a basket and took him to the river. She told Miriam to hide behind the bushes and watch him. This was a huge responsibility for a young girl, but Miriam knew how the midwives and her mother and daddy trusted and obeyed God. I'm sure Miriam knew about God's promise, and so she trusted Him too. And then it happened! The princess of the land went to the river to bathe. Susie, read Exodus 2:5-6."

Susie read, "'She saw the basket among the reeds and sent her slave girl to get it. She opened it and saw the baby. He was crying, and she felt sorry for him'" (Exodus 2:5-6 NIV).

Pastor Scotty continued, "Who do you think caused the princess to see the basket? Who do you think caused her to feel sorry for the baby?"

"God!" shouted all the kids.

"Touchdown!" yelled Pastor Scotty. "The sovereign God watched over the baby, and then God gave the big sister wisdom to know exactly what to do. Miriam skipped up to the princess and said, 'Would you like for me to get one of the Israelite women to care for the baby for you?' The princess liked Miriam's idea. Miriam ran and got her mother. When Jocebed arrived, the princess said, 'Take this baby and nurse him for me, and I will pay you.'"

"I love this part!" Cassie declared. "Jocebed was able to take care of her own baby, and she was even paid for doing it."

Pastor Scotty laughed. "The princess named the baby Moses. Four hundred years earlier God had promised Abraham that He would deliver the Israelites out of Egypt. That's a long time to wait. Sometimes it may seem that God has forgotten His promise, but God never forgets. He is always with us, He is always in control of everything that happens, and He always keeps all of His promises. At just the right time God sent a little baby into the world to deliver the Israelites out of Egypt and take them home to Israel."

"Pastor Scotty!" exclaimed Mac. "I think we can learn something else from this. At just the right time God kept His promise and sent baby Jesus into the world to deliver us from our sin so that we can go home to heaven and live with Him forever."

Pastor Scotty threw his arms up, and all the kids shouted, "Touchdown!"

"I love you kids!" he said. "Teaching you is better than scoring the game-winning touchdown in the Super Bowl!"

LET'S TALK

What did God say would happen to Abraham's family?

How long did God say they would be slaves in Egypt?

What did God say He would do after four hundred years?

What is something we learn about God in this story?

Because God keeps His promises, what should we do?

How did God keep His promise to deliver us from sin?

What do you learn about Jesus in this story? (Read Galatians 4:4.)

CHAPTER SIX

How Do We Know?

———— ■ ————

COVENANT PRIVILEGE AND RESPONSIBILITY: TRUST

Some trust in chariots and some in horses, but we trust in the name of the Lord our God. (Psalm 20:7 NIV)

Pastor Scotty was waiting on the sideline when Angus finished soccer practice. "Hi, Dad. This is Amin Al-Jafir. His family just moved here, and he's on my team."

Amin's parents joined them, and Pastor Scotty introduced himself. Later, as they drove home, Angus asked, "Dad, why did Amin's mom have on that long dress, and why was her face covered with that cloth?"

"That's called a burkah. Amin and his family are Muslims."

"Do you mean that Amin is not a Christian?" asked Angus.

"That's right, son."

"But I really like him. Can I still be his friend?"

"Absolutely!" replied Pastor Scotty. "We are to show the love of Jesus to everyone, and we are to pray that they will turn from their false god and trust in Jesus."

A few days later Angus asked his mom why their neighbors, Mr. and Mrs. Seelig, went to church on Saturday. She explained, "They're Jewish. They don't believe that Jesus is the Savior; so they still celebrate the Sabbath on Saturday like people did before Jesus rose from the dead on a Sunday."

"Do you mean that Mr. and Mrs. Seelig aren't Christians?" asked Angus.

His mom nodded.

"But they're so kind to all the kids in the neighborhood, and I love them!" moaned Angus.

Angus walked slowly outside and climbed up in his tree house. He had a lot to think about, and his tree house was his thinking place. Later he heard his dad's voice. "Hi, Angus. Is it okay if I come up and join you?"

"Sure, Dad."

Pastor Scotty could barely squeeze his long arms and legs into the tree house. Angus smiled as his dad scrunched his big body into the small space. "You seem troubled, Angus. Is anything wrong?"

"Well, I've been wondering about something," began Angus cautiously. "I really like Amin, and I love Mr. and Mrs. Seelig, but they're not Christians."

Pastor Scotty looked tenderly at his son. "I understand. You're concerned about their salvation. I'm thankful that you care about them, Angus."

Angus put his head in his hands and didn't say anything. His dad asked, "Is anything else bothering you?"

Angus looked up at him, and his eyes were filled with tears. "Dad, I do care about them, and I do want them to become Christians, but . . ."

"What is it, son?"

"Well . . . Dad, how do we know that we're right? They think they're right too. How can we be sure that what we believe is true?" Angus put his head in his hands again. "Are you mad at me, Dad? Do you think I'm terrible for thinking this?"

"Angus, it's great that you're thinking about such a big question. I didn't start thinking about this until I was a teenager."

"Do you mean that you've wondered about this too?" asked Angus.

"Sure, and thinking about this question will help you to grow in your faith and to trust God even more. Let's go inside and get our Bibles."

Angus felt as if a heavy load was lifted from him. When they were settled on the couch, Pastor Scotty began. "Angus, every religion in the world, except Christianity, tells people what they must do to go to heaven. The Bible tells us what God has done for us so that we can go to heaven. The question is not who is right and who is wrong, but what is truth? Read John 17:17."

Angus read: "'Sanctify them in the truth; your word is truth'" (NIV).

Pastor Scotty explained, "This is Jesus' prayer for us. Now read what Jesus said in John 16:13."

Angus read: "'When the Spirit of truth comes, he will guide you into all the truth.'"

Pastor Scotty continued, "God's Word is truth. God's Spirit lives in His children and gives us power to believe God's Word. Angus, there will be other times in your life when you need to be sure of your faith. Ask the Holy Spirit to guide you so that you will know the truth, and ask Him to help you to obey His truth."

Angus and his dad prayed. Then Angus said, "Thanks, Dad. I'm glad it's okay to have questions."

"It's great to have questions," boomed Pastor Scotty. "Just remember to take your questions to the Lord. Search His Word and ask the Holy Spirit to teach you. God has also given us other Christians to teach and encourage us. I'm going to visit Sir John. He's been sick, and I want to see how he's feeling. Would you like to go with me?"

"Sure," grinned Angus.

Miss Jenny greeted them at the door. "I'm glad you came to see Papa. He's better today, and he'll enjoy a visit. Come in and sit down, and I'll go fetch some shortbread and milk." Miss Jenny scurried off as Angus hugged Sir John.

Pastor Scotty told Sir John about Angus's question. "Sir John, what would you say to a young fellow like Angus to help him know that what we believe is true?"

Sir John looked intently at Angus. His eyes twinkled. "Ah, laddie, I have lived a heap o' years. I'm an old man. I don't know how much longer I have left on this earth, but each day I'm more confident that God's Word is true and that He keeps every promise. I know that He loved the world so much that He sent His Son to die for our sins. Every day heaven becomes more real to me than the things I can see and touch and hear on this earth. Every day I'm more confident that He will never leave me and that He will take me safely home to heaven. When I was a wee lad, my father taught me Psalm 20:7. I encourage you to memorize it." Sir John closed his eyes and said with gusto, "'Some trust in chariots and some in horses, but we trust in the name of the LORD our God.'"

The old man, the young pastor, and the little boy prayed. Then Miss Jenny returned with refreshments. When Pastor Scotty and Angus left, Angus looked the same size on the outside, but he had grown about ten feet spiritually.

LET'S TALK

Why was Angus troubled?

What was his big question?

Who gives us power to know that God's Word is true?

What did Sir John tell Angus?

CHAPTER SEVEN

Is It Time?

■

COVENANT PRIVILEGE AND RESPONSIBILITY: TRUST

Some trust in chariots and some in horses, but we trust in the name
of the Lord our God. (Psalm 20:7 NIV)

Susie put her hands on her hips, cocked her head, and asked her parents, "When are you going to China?"

Her mom looked at her dad. "It's your turn to answer her."

Just at that moment Angus bounded down the stairs. "Is it time for you to go to China to get my baby sister?"

Pastor Scotty threw up his hands, pretending to be exasperated. "We need a family meeting."

The family gathered around the kitchen table. Pastor Scotty opened the desk drawer and took out their missionary map that they used to pray for missionaries all over the world. Angus and Susie were grinning because they were sure their parents were finally going to tell them that they were off to China.

"Angus and Susie, there are some things you need to understand about adopting a baby," Pastor Scotty began as he unfolded the map. "First, we live here." He pointed to the map. "That's right—in the USA!" Susie sang.

"And China is *waaay* over here." Pastor Scotty pointed on the map.

"Right, so when are you leaving?" Angus pressed.

"It's a very long airplane trip, and long airplane trips are expensive," Pastor Scotty continued.

"And there are a lot of other expenses involved with adopting a baby," added their mom.

"Okay, we get it. It's expensive," Susie said a little impatiently. "So when are you leaving?"

"We have no idea," Pastor Scotty declared. "We have to save a lot of money."

"Well, why don't we just get a baby who is not so far away so we won't need so much money?" asked Susie.

"Now that's a good question. We've prayed about this for a long time. Of course there are children all over the world who need a loving home, but God has burdened our hearts for the little girls in China who have been orphaned or abandoned. Kids, we don't have much money, but we are rich in love. So we trust God to provide the money."

Their mom looked at them tenderly. "The Lord has blessed us with two wonderful children who also have a lot of love to give. We believe you two are strong enough in your faith to make the sacrifices necessary for us to adopt a child."

"I have an idea!" Angus beamed. "On television when they need money, they just use a credit card. Do you have a credit card, Dad?"

"Angus," Pastor Scotty laughed, "a credit card is not the answer! And I'll have a lot more to say about that when you're older. But for now, I want you to remember, 'Some trust in chariots and some in horses'—and some trust in credit cards—'but we trust in the name of the LORD our God.'"

"Well," continued Angus, "maybe we could enter a contest and win some money."

His dad looked at him but didn't say a word.

"Oh," blurted Angus. "What was I thinking? 'Some trust in chariots and some in horses'—and some trust in contests to win money—'but we trust in the name of the LORD our God.'"

His dad gave him a high five.

Susie had a worried look on her face. "But what if someone else adopts our baby before we get enough money? What if the people in charge give her to another family?"

"Another good question," responded her dad. "God is sovereign. He's completely in control. He'll arrange everything so that the baby He wants us to adopt will be there at the very time we have the money. If the money doesn't come quickly, maybe it's because our baby has not even been born. Remember, 'Some trust in chariots and some in horses'—and some trust in their own schedules or in the people in charge—'but we trust in the name of the LORD our God.'"

Angus, the thinker, listened carefully to everything his dad said. Suddenly it was as if he was connecting dots in his brain. "I've got it!" he blurted out. "This is just like the midwives and Moses' family. They trusted and obeyed God, and God used them to work out His plan for baby Moses. We can trust God to work our His plan for our baby!"

"Wow," said an awestruck Susie. "God had a great plan for Moses. I wonder what His plan is for our baby."

"And I wonder what His plan is for our baby's big brother and sister." Their mom smiled.

LET'S TALK

Why did Pastor Scotty and his wife want to adopt a baby from China?

What did they need?

Why wasn't Pastor Scotty worried that someone else would adopt their baby before they had enough money?

What did Angus finally realize?

CHAPTER EIGHT

A Caring Covenant Family

◼

COVENANT PRIVILEGE AND RESPONSIBILITY: TRUST

*Some trust in chariots and some in horses, but we trust in the name
of the Lord our God. (Psalm 20:7 NIV)*

"I have an idea for a way to save money to adopt a baby!" exclaimed Susie.

Pastor Scotty laughed. "Let's hope it's better than those doozies you came up with at breakfast. I just don't think I can stand at the back of the church with a diaper bag and ask people to drop in their loose change."

"And I definitely don't think we can turn our house into a hotel," added Heather.

Angus frowned. "Well, those weren't as bad as Dad's idea to hire Susie and me out to clean people's houses. But I do have another idea. We can put on a daredevil show and charge people admission! We could borrow some school buses, and I could jump over them on my skateboard! And I could ride wheelies on my bicycle and do tricks on my scooter!"

Susie gave her brother an exasperated look. "Angus! You don't know how to do any tricks, and you sure can't jump over a school bus on your skateboard!"

"I guess you're right," Angus admitted. "But it would be really cool."

"I have a *serious* idea," insisted Susie. "Why don't we put a big jar on the table, and whenever we save money on something, we can put it in the jar."

"Now that's a good idea," agreed her dad.

Susie chattered on about which jar they should use and finally decided that she could decorate a special jar. Angus was quiet.

Finally his mom asked, "Angus, is something wrong?"

"Well, I'm a little confused. Are we trusting God if we save our money?"

"Good question!" said his dad. "God provides for us, but He tells us to be good stewards of everything He gives us. It's right for us to ask Him to help us use our money wisely. It would be wrong for us to be wasteful and to expect God to give us the money."

A couple days later Pastor Scotty asked, "Who wants to go out to eat tonight?"

"I do!" said Angus.

"I do too!" agreed his mom.

Pastor Scotty looked at Susie. "How about you, little girl?"

"Well," replied Susie slowly, "why don't we stay home and put that money in our jar?"

Her parents looked at each other. They really wanted to go to a restaurant and have someone wait on them for a change. Pastor Scotty knew that his wife had been busy that day and had not started preparing dinner. "Your call," he told her.

After a long pause she said, "Susie's right. Staying home would be the best thing to do."

"I have another good idea," grinned Susie. "Dad and I will make fancy peanut butter and jelly sandwiches for everyone. Mom, you go stretch out on the couch."

"That's my girl," said her mom as she waltzed to the couch.

"Wait a minute! How do you make fancy peanut butter and jelly sandwiches?" asked Dad.

"Easy. You cut the crust off the bread, put a cherry on top of the sandwich, and put candles on the table," answered Susie.

A few weeks later Pastor Scotty startled everyone when he burst in and announced, "I've got big news! You know that everyone at church has been praying with us about adopting a baby. Some of them decided they wanted to help, and so they had a huge yard sale. Today they gave me this check. We now have over half the money we need!"

"Why would they do that?" asked Susie.

"Because a covenant family cares for each other," answered Heather.

"Let's thank the Lord!" proclaimed Angus.

And that is exactly what they did.

A few weeks later Pastor Scotty was looking through the mail when suddenly he stopped. "What's this?" He opened an envelope and took out a stack of money. He looked in the envelope again. "There's no return address. The note says, 'For the baby—from your covenant family.'" He quickly counted the money. His lip quivered as he said, "We almost have enough."

"Exactly how much more do we need?" asked Heather slowly.

"Let me do the math," her husband replied. Angus handed him a calculator.

Pastor Scotty punched in the numbers. "Drum roll please—we need $1,000."

Heather gasped. They all looked at her. "I was going to tell you all at dinner. Mom and Dad called today and said they put a check in the mail for $1,000."

They sat in stunned silence for a few moments, and then Angus began reciting Psalm 20:7. Everyone joined him: "'Some trust in chariots and some in horses, but we trust in the name of the LORD our God.'"

■

LET'S TALK

What were some of the silly ideas the family had to get money?

What was Susie's good idea?

How did God provide money for the adoption?

CHAPTER NINE

Glory Story—God Is with Us

EXODUS 2—5

■

A COVENANT PROMISE:

*I will be with you. . . . go, and I will be with your mouth and teach you what
you shall speak. (Exodus 3:12; 4:12)*

A COVENANT PRIVILEGE AND RESPONSIBILITY: HUMILITY

*. . . younger people, submit yourselves to your elders. . . . and be clothed
with humility, for "God resists the proud, but gives grace to the humble."
(1 Peter 5:5 NKJV)*

Pastor Scotty watched the kids arrive for Covenant Kids Club. This is one of the most important things I do. I love these covenant kids, and I love teaching them God's Word, he thought to himself.

When the kids were settled in their chairs, he blew his whistle and shouted, "Covenant kids, you're part of God's covenant family, and I want you to know your family history! Do you want to know your family history?"

"Yes, sir!" yelled the kids.

Pastor Scotty continued, "Remember—our history is not about dead people. It's about how God makes His people holy and blameless so that we can live in His presence. The people we talk about are living in His presence right now! Their bodies have died, but their souls are with Jesus! Turn in your Bibles to Numbers 12:3 and tell me what kind of man Moses was."

"I've got it," said Caleb. "'Now Moses was a very humble man, more humble than anyone else on the face of the earth'" (NIV).

"What does humble mean?" asked Cassie.

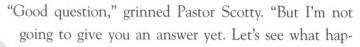

"Good question," grinned Pastor Scotty. "But I'm not going to give you an answer yet. Let's see what happened to Moses, and then I think you'll understand what it means to be humble. Moses grew up in the palace as the son of Pharaoh's daughter. I guess he thought he was *somebody* special! One day he saw an Egyptian beating an Israelite. Moses didn't stop and ask God what he should do. He killed the Egyptian. Pharaoh found out what Moses had done and tried to kill him; so Moses left Egypt quicker than I can say 'touchdown.' He spent the next forty years in the desert taking care of sheep.

Well, that's a switch—from the palace to the desert. But that is exactly what God had planned. Moses needed to be brought down a notch or two. Moses needed to learn humility. Finally Moses was ready. One day an amazing thing happened. Does anyone know what Moses saw?"

Every hand went up, and every child said, "A burning bush that didn't burn up!"

Pastor Scotty held his arms up and yelled, "Touchdown!"

"Now, kids," he said, "let's hunker down and see if we can learn what this burning bush was all about. Caleb, read Exodus 3:4-6."

Caleb read, " '. . . God called to him out of the bush, "Moses, Moses!" And he said, "Here I am." Then he said, "Do not come near; take your sandals off your feet, for the place on which you are standing is holy ground." And he said, "I am the God of your father, the God of Abraham, the God of Isaac, and the God of Jacob." ' "

"Did you hear that?" asked Pastor Scotty. "God said, I *am* the God of Abraham, Isaac, and Jacob. Those guys had been dead for years! Why didn't He say, I *was* their God?"

Angus grinned and tried to sound just like his dad. "Because our history is not about dead people. Their bodies died, but their souls are with Jesus! And when we go to heaven, we'll be able to talk to them."

All the kids covered their ears as Pastor Scotty shouted, "Touchdown!"

When the cheering stopped, Pastor Scotty asked Susie to read verses 7, 8, and 10.

Susie read, "'Then the LORD said, "I have surely seen the affliction of my people who are in Egypt. . . . I know their sufferings, and I have come down to deliver them out of the hand of the Egyptians. . . . Come, I will send you to Pharaoh that you may bring my people, the children of Israel, out of Egypt.'"

Pastor Scotty explained, "God had promised to deliver His children out of Egypt, and He called Moses to be the deliverer. Forty years earlier, when Moses was living in the palace, he probably would have said, 'I'm your man! I'll take charge. No problem!' But Moses had spent forty years in the desert. Moses had learned that he wasn't such a hotshot. Daniel, read verse 11."

Daniel read, "'But Moses said to God, "Who am I that I should go to Pharaoh and bring the children of Israel out of Egypt?"'"

Pastor Scotty said, "Moses was no longer proud. When Moses admitted that he could not lead God's people in his own strength, what did God tell him? Cassie, read verse 12."

Cassie read, "'I will be with you. . . .'"

Pastor Scotty continued, "Then Moses asked God what he should say if the people asked him who sent him. God told Moses to tell the people, 'I AM WHO I AM.'"

"What did that mean?" asked one of the children.

"This name meant that God is eternal. He did not have a beginning, and He will not have an end. Just as the burning bush did not burn up, so God will never end. But Moses was still afraid he couldn't do it. He said, 'Lord, I can't go to Pharaoh. I'm not a good speaker.' Caleb, read 5:11-12 to find out what God told Moses."

Caleb read, "The LORD said to him, 'Who gave man his mouth? . . . Is it not I, the LORD? Now go; I will help you speak and will teach you what to say'" (NIV).

Pastor Scotty had the serious look on his face. The kids listened carefully. "God promised the one thing that Moses needed. God promised to be with him. Moses did not have to depend on his own ability. God made his mouth, and God would teach him what to say. When Moses realized that he was weak and that he needed God, then Moses became strong. A humble person does not trust in himself. He trusts God, and he depends on God. He is teachable. He wants God's will to be done, and he wants God to teach him how to do it. He believes that God is with him; so he is not afraid to do what God tells him to do."

"Pastor Scotty," exclaimed Caleb, "that reminds me of what Jesus said before He went back to heaven! He said for us to go into all the world and tell people about Him, and then He said, '. . . I am with you always, to the end of the age'" (Matthew 28:19-20).

"Here it comes!" yelled Daniel just as Pastor Scotty shouted, "Touchdown!"

■

LET'S TALK

What did Moses see in the desert?

What did God tell Moses to do?

What did God promise?

God told Moses that His name is I AM. Read John 8:58 to see what Jesus said.

What did Jesus promise before He went back to heaven? (Read Matthew 28:19-20.)

Because God is always with us, and it is His power that enables us to do what He tells us to do, what should our attitude be?

CHAPTER TEN

The Attic

■

COVENANT PRIVILEGE AND RESPONSIBILITY: HUMILITY

. . . younger people, submit yourselves to your elders. . . . and be clothed with humility, for "God resists the proud, but gives grace to the humble."
(1 Peter 5:5 NKJV)

Cassie and Mary were playing with their baby dolls when Granny Grace peeped into Mary's room. "Girls, would you like to go to The Attic and make some clothes for your dolls?"

"Yes, ma'am!"

The girls followed Granny Grace to The Attic. It's really not an attic, but Granny Grace calls it that because it's stuffed with her stuff. There's a sewing machine, a table to do craft projects, big boxes of fabric, little boxes of buttons, ribbon, crayons, stacks of construction paper, and piles of drawing paper.

"I love this place," murmured Cassie.

Soon each girl had chosen a piece of fabric, and they watched with amazement as Granny Grace cut and stitched. The girls asked a zillion questions. "Why do you pin the pattern to the cloth? How do you know which pieces to put together? Will it fit my doll?"

Granny Grace laughed and patiently answered their questions.

When the clothes were almost finished, Cassie asked, "Granny Grace, how do you know how to do all of this? I don't think I'll ever be able to sew."

Granny Grace's eyes twinkled. "I guess I know how because I've lived a long time, and many people have taught me many things. So the point is that you girls can learn a lot if you're teachable and if you listen to old folks like me!" Then she held up the two doll dresses.

"They're beautiful! May we put them on our dolls?" asked Cassie breathlessly.

As the girls dressed their dolls, Mary said, "This reminds me of our memory verse."

"What is your memory verse?" asked Granny Grace.

The girls recited, ". . . younger people, submit yourselves to your elders. . . . and be clothed with humility, for 'God resists the proud, but gives grace to the humble' (1 Peter 5:5)."

Mary continued, "We listened to you, and now we are clothing our dolls!"

Cassie looked puzzled. "Granny Grace, how can we be clothed with humility?"

Granny Grace thought for a minute and then jumped up and spread two pieces of butcher paper on the floor. She told the girls to lie on the paper, and she outlined their bodies. "Now we'll name our little girls. Mary, let's name yours Humble Helen. Cassie, yours is Proud Paula." The girls wrote the names on their papers.

Granny Grace told them to draw a heart on their girls as she explained, "Clothing ourselves with humility begins on the inside. Proud Paula's heart is filled with herself."

Cassie wrote "Self" on the heart.

Granny Grace continued, "We cannot make our hearts humble. When Jesus gives us a new heart, He frees us from slavery to sin so that we can do what is good in His sight."

"That's like the Israelites," said Cassie. "God freed them from slavery in Egypt."

"That's right!" exclaimed Granny Grace. "We must ask Jesus to deliver us from the sin of pride and to give us humble hearts. Humble Helen prayed that her heart would be empty of herself and filled with Jesus."

Mary wrote "Jesus" on the heart.

Granny Grace continued, "Our behavior will show what's in our hearts. When our hearts are filled with Jesus, He changes the way we act on the outside. Our actions are like clothes. So let's draw some clothes on our girls that show what is in their hearts. Proud Paula's heart is full of herself; so what kind of actions do you think she will wear?"

"I think I understand what you mean!" exclaimed Mary as she began drawing.

"I get it too," squealed Cassie, and she grabbed some markers.

Soon the girls had finished, and they were ready to show their outfits.

Cassie began, "Proud Paula has a dirty, ragged dress—selfishness, pride, disobedience."

Mary pointed to her drawing. On one sleeve she had written "teachable," and on the other "obedient." Her skirt had two little flowers with four petals each. The petals spelled "love" and "kind." Humble Helen had on a necklace with beads that spelled "humility."

Granny Grace clapped her hands. "This is wonderful! You girls are so creative. May I use your drawings with the three-year-olds in my Sunday school class?"

"Sure," beamed Mary and Cassie.

"Umm," Mary remarked, "we are the elders, and we're teaching the younger children."

"You're exactly right!" responded Granny Grace. "Everyone in the covenant family needs to care for and teach those who are younger, even as we learn from those who are older. But it all starts with humble hearts that are empty of self and filled with Jesus."

———■———

LET'S TALK

Does being clothed with humility begin on the inside or the outside?

What kind of heart did Proud Paula have?

What did her clothes look like?

What kind of heart did Humble Helen have?

What did her clothes look like?

How do we get a humble heart?

CHAPTER ELEVEN

Puffed with Pride

■

COVENANT PRIVILEGE AND RESPONSIBILITY: HUMILITY

. . . younger people, submit yourselves to your elders. . . . and be clothed with humility, for "God resists the proud, but gives grace to the humble."
(1 Peter 5:5 NKJV)

Caleb yawned and stretched as he rolled over in bed. He was only half awake, but he started grinning as he thought about the night before when the family played games. "I'm so good at board games. I won almost every game."

After he had gotten dressed, he passed Cassie in the hall. "Hi, Cass. Are you still pouting because I beat you in every game?" he laughed. Caleb was very competitive, and he loved to win.

He sat down for breakfast and announced, "This is the day. This afternoon is the music competition. I'm sure I'll win best trumpet. Do you all want to congratulate me now?"

"Caleb," said his mom, "you haven't been practicing regularly. Are you sure you still want to enter the competition?"

"Sure. I don't need to practice every day."

Recently Caleb had won bicycle races in the neighborhood and made it to level nine in his new video game. He was always the highest scorer on his basketball team. The problem was that Caleb had become puffed up with pride.

When they arrived at the music competition, Cassie was nervous. "Could we pray before we go in? Please pray that I will remember the music and that my violin won't squeak."

"Sure, Cassie," answered her dad. "Caleb, do you want us to pray for you?"

"I guess so," he replied.

Cassie played first, and she remembered every note. She had practiced hard and prayed hard.

Then it was Caleb's turn. He confidently strolled across the stage, put his trumpet to his mouth, and played the first five notes. But he couldn't remember the next note. He started over, but he still couldn't remember. He felt the blood rush to his head. He tried to start over a third time, but his mind was blank. He didn't know what to do. The judge suggested that Caleb come back later and try again.

"Thank you, sir," Caleb said, "but I don't think I could do any better. I'm really not prepared. I'm sorry." He walked off the stage.

His dad was there to meet him. "Let's go for a walk, son."

After they had walked awhile in silence, Caleb spoke. "Dad, I've been pretty cocky, haven't I?"

"Yep," replied his dad.

"I deserved what happened today, didn't I?"

"Umm," responded his dad. "I don't know what you deserved, but maybe you needed something like this. Do you remember our memory verse?"

Caleb nodded and recited, ". . . younger people, submit yourselves to your elders. . . . and be clothed with humility, for 'God resists the proud, but gives grace to the humble.'" He looked at his dad. "You're old; so will you tell me what I need to learn from all of this?"

"What do you mean, old?" laughed his dad. Then he became serious. "Actually, Caleb, asking that question is a good start. Humility means that we're teachable. When we're proud, we think we know it all and that we don't need others. We just think about ourselves rather than what is good for others. Last night when we played board games, all you thought about was winning. You didn't notice that your little sister was discouraged. Today you depended on yourself. You didn't think you needed to practice, and you didn't think you needed to depend on the Lord."

"What should I do?" asked Caleb.

"It begins in your heart," explained his dad. "You must recognize pride as sin and ask the Lord to forgive you and to give you a humble heart."

Saturday morning Cassie and Caleb hurried to the kitchen for the Saturday morning special—waffles. Caleb already had on his uniform for his basketball game. He was quiet during breakfast.

"Caleb, is anything wrong?" asked his mom.

"It's the pride thing," he answered. "I don't want to be proud, but you know that I usually score the most points on our team. Should I not play good so I won't seem proud? Is it wrong to win?"

"It's great to win!" exclaimed his dad. "Caleb, God has given you the ability to be a good basketball player. You should play the best you can for His glory. Ask Him to take off any pride, like a piece of dirty clothing, and show you how to glorify Him."

Caleb's team gathered in the locker room. The coach waited a moment until he had their attention. "Boys, we're playing the Hornets, and they're good. Play hard, and whenever possible pass the ball to Caleb. He's our best chance of winning."

In the past, Caleb would have stuck out his chest and grinned, but he felt uncomfortable when everyone started chanting, "Go, Caleb; go, Caleb."

He prayed silently, "Lord, help me not to be proud. Show me how to play for Your glory."

When the game started, Caleb immediately scored a few baskets. Instead of jumping around and celebrating, he ran back down the court and got into position to play defense. Caleb scored almost every time he got the ball. During the second half, his team gained a big lead. Then Caleb got the ball again, dribbled down the court, and was in position to shoot when he turned and passed the ball to one of his teammates who had not scored. The boy was so shocked that he didn't score, but Caleb yelled, "Good try." The next time Caleb got the ball, he did the same thing, and this time the boy scored. Caleb was more excited than his teammate. Caleb continued to do this for the rest of the game.

When the game was over, his dad ran out to meet him on the court. "Caleb, you figured it out! You played a great game, and you thought about the others on your team. I know it took every ounce of strength in you not to shoot the ball yourself. How did you do it?"

"I just kept praying, Dad. God put it in my heart to want the others to score."

"Caleb, that's the best game you've ever played." His dad grinned. "But let's be absolutely sure you have this straight. If your team had been behind, what should you have done?"

Caleb laughed. "I know, Dad. I should have kept the ball and scored."

———■———

LET'S TALK

What are some of the things pride caused Caleb to do?

What did Caleb's dad tell him he needed to do about his prideful heart?

What did Caleb do during the basketball game?

Is it wrong to be good at something?

CHAPTER TWELVE

Mayday!

COVENANT PRIVILEGE AND RESPONSIBILITY: HUMILITY

. . . younger people, submit yourselves to your elders. . . . and be clothed with humility, for "God resists the proud, but gives grace to the humble."
(1 Peter 5:5 NKJV)

"Papa Sam and Mama Maggie are coming home tomorrow!" Angus announced to everyone at Covenant Kids Club. Suddenly the playground was buzzing with excitement. Even though the travelers were Pastor Scotty's parents, all the kids at church called them Papa Sam and Mama Maggie. Angus and Susie were glad to share their grandparents with everyone else.

"Do you think they'll have pictures?" asked Cassie.

"Did they have any wild adventures in the jungle?" asked Daniel.

Papa Sam was a retired air force fighter pilot. He and Mama Maggie went on several mission trips each year. They always came back with exciting stories.

The following week Papa Sam took Angus, Caleb, Daniel, and Mac to an air show. The boys couldn't believe their eyes. There were airplanes everywhere. There were big planes, small planes, military fighter planes, helicopters, and stunt planes. As they walked around, Papa Sam told the boys about the airplanes. "Boys, this plane is called a Corsair." Papa Sam showed them a World War II era plane. "And this one is a Mustang."

"Is that what you flew?" asked Angus.

"No, that was before my time. This is what I flew!" he said, pointing to a beautiful airplane.

"Wow!" the boys all said together.

"Do you notice anything different about this airplane?" Papa Sam quizzed.

"Yes, sir. It doesn't have a propeller!" exclaimed Daniel.

"Right!" grinned Papa Sam. "This is an F9F Panther. The Korean War was the first time that jets were used in combat."

"Did you go on combat missions?" asked Mac.

"Yes, I did. I usually escorted the huge B-29s and occasionally bombed airfields or railroad tracks."

"Cool!" the boys said all together.

"When I grow up, I'm going to be a fighter pilot," declared Daniel.

"Me too," Angus chimed in.

"I'm going to fly a fighter helicopter with the big guns on the side," announced Mac.

"I want to fly the F9F Panthers, just like Papa Sam!" said Caleb.

"Whoa, buckaroos!" exclaimed Papa Sam. "You boys are forgetting something."

"What?" they all asked at the same time.

"God made each one of you with specific abilities to do what He planned for you to do before the creation of the world. I'm hearing a lot of 'I'm gonna' from you boys. Maybe you need to humble yourselves and ask the Lord what He wants you to do. He may want you to be a fighter pilot, but the important thing is to seek His will and to follow Him. Would you like to hear my mayday story?"

"Yes, sir!" answered the boys. They loved Papa Sam's stories.

"When I was a fighter pilot, we all had call signs—that's like a nickname. Mine was Boss."

"Why were you called that?" asked Daniel.

"Because I was so stubborn and cocky. I always wanted my own way. I wanted to be in control, and I would never admit that I needed help. I thought I knew more than anyone else."

"But, Papa Sam, you're not cocky," protested Daniel.

"I was before I knew the Lord Jesus. One of the other pilots in the squadron was a Christian. His call sign was Preacher. He tried to talk to me about the Lord, but I made fun of him. I believed there was a God, but I thought I was a good person, and so I was sure I would go to heaven. Preacher tried to explain that the only way I could be saved was to repent of my sin and depend on Jesus. I would get so angry that I would walk away.

"Then one day I was given orders to fly a long and dangerous mission. I took off from the aircraft carrier and had just enough fuel to get to my destination. About three hours into the flight a bad fog rolled in. I couldn't see a thing. Then my instruments went crazy. In those days we didn't have the technology they have today. Before long, I realized I was lost. I kept thinking that I would come out of the fog and get my bearings. I didn't want to radio for help."

"Why?" asked an astonished Mac. "Weren't you scared?"

"Sure, but I didn't want to admit that I was lost."

"Oh—the pride problem," said Mac.

"Exactly," replied Papa Sam. "I was totally disoriented. Then I looked at my fuel gauge and realized that I was in serious trouble."

"What did you do?" asked Daniel.

"I grabbed my radio and yelled, 'MAYDAY! MAYDAY!'"

Papa Sam yelled so loudly that the boys jumped. "The voice on the radio came back: 'I'm in your vicinity. I can see the fog. I'm coming in to find you.'"

Papa Sam clenched his teeth. "It was Preacher. I was furious. I didn't want to have to depend on anyone to help me, especially Preacher. Then I looked at the fuel gauge again, and I knew that I was in a desperate situation. In a few seconds Preacher's voice came over my radio. 'I have you in my sights. I'm coming up beside you. Get on my wing.'"

"What does that mean?" asked a wide-eyed Angus. "Did you have to get out of your plane and get on his wing?"

Papa Sam grinned. "In this maneuver, the pilot whose instruments are not working has to fly so close to the other plane that their wings are just about five feet apart. You have to follow the other pilot down and trust him completely to get you on the ground. You have to keep your eyes on his wing. It would be disastrous if you begin to think that you know a better way."

"Is it scary to trust someone else that much?" asked Mac.

"Yep," replied Papa Sam. "But when you realize that you're lost and helpless, it's scarier to trust yourself. When we landed, I swallowed my pride and thanked Preacher for rescuing me. Later he pointed out that if I had just believed that he was there but refused to trust him and get on his wing, I would have crashed. He told me that just believing there is a God would not get me to heaven. I had to humble myself and admit that I could never be good enough to get to heaven on my own. God gave me a new heart. I realized my desperate situation without a Savior, and I trusted Jesus."

"So did you change your name since you weren't prideful anymore?" asked Caleb.

"No, I kept the name to remind myself of my tendency to want to be in control and to do things my way. I wish I could say that I never have a pride problem now, but the truth is that I struggle with it every day. But the more I know of God's power and love, the more I depend on Him. Every morning I pray, 'Mayday! I need you, Lord. Help me to follow You.'"

LET'S TALK

What was Papa Sam's call sign when he was a pilot? Explain why.

How did he think he could go to heaven?

When Papa Sam was lost, why didn't he want to call for help?

How does one pilot get on another pilot's wing?

What did this help Papa Sam understand?

CHAPTER THIRTEEN

Glory Story—God Redeems His People

EXODUS 5—7

■

A COVENANT PROMISE:

I will redeem you with an outstretched arm. . . . I will take you to be my people, and I will be your God. (Exodus 6:6-7)

A COVENANT PRIVILEGE AND RESPONSIBILITY: WORSHIP

Therefore, since we are receiving a kingdom that cannot be shaken, let us be thankful, and so worship God acceptably with reverence and awe.
(Hebrews 12:28 NIV)

Pastor Scotty blew his whistle, and immediately everyone was silent. "I love this job—and I love you kids. You belong to your parents, but you also belong to our covenant family. So you belong to me!"

"I love to belong," Cassie cooed.

Pastor Scotty laughed. "I do too. And speaking of belonging, turn to Exodus 5:1. What did God tell Moses to tell Pharaoh?"

Pages turned, and then several children answered, "Let My people go."

Pastor Scotty continued, "Pharaoh thought the Israelites were his slaves, but God said, 'These are My people. They belong to Me.' Pharaoh resisted God. He did not let the people go but made them work even harder. Then the people were angry with Moses. Isn't that just like us? When things don't go our way, we start complaining and whining. But God said, 'I have heard the groaning of the Israelites, and I have remembered my covenant.' Then God told Moses seven things He would do for His people. Look at Exodus 6:6-8 and see if you can find them."

Mary raised her hand. "He would bring them out from under the yoke of the Egyptians."

Other voices called out:

"He would free them from being slaves."

"He would redeem them."

"He would take them as His own people."

"He would be their God."

"He would bring them to the land He promised to Abraham, Isaac, and Jacob."

"And number seven," exclaimed Caleb, "He would give them the land!"

"Touchdown! You'll score the extra point if you can tell me *why* God let things get hard for the Israelites."

Everyone looked at the verses again. Then Mac jumped up. "I see it. 'Then you will know that I am the LORD your God, who brought you out from under the yoke of the Egyptians'" (NIV).

"Score!" yelled Pastor Scotty. He got his serious look on his face, and everyone listened carefully. "God could have caused Pharaoh to say, 'Sure, they can go.' But God was working everything out to accomplish His purpose. He wanted His people to know that He was their God. When the Israelites left Egypt, God wanted them to know that it was because He redeemed them by His power."

"I think I get it," said Mary. "Sometimes hard things happen so that we will learn more about God."

Immediately all of the kids covered their ears because they knew what was coming.

"Touchdown!" yelled Pastor Scotty. The kids laughed as he did his victory dance. When he calmed down, he continued, "God told Moses to go back to Pharaoh. Daniel, read Exodus 7:16 to find out why God wanted the people to leave Egypt."

Daniel read, "'Let my people go, so that they may worship me in the desert.'"

"But, Pastor Scotty, why was it such a big deal for the people to go out in the desert and have a worship service?" asked Mac.

"Worship is not just a service we attend on Sunday. Worship is the way we live. We worship the one we love 24/7. Everything we do, every minute of the day, shows who or what we worship. Now do you see why God let things get hard for His people?"

There was silence. Pastor Scotty grinned. "I'll tell you. This was not just a struggle between Moses and Pharaoh. This was a battle between God and Satan. God was going to redeem His people so that they would be free to live with Him in a holy relationship. God wanted His people to learn more about His power and His love. He wanted them to know Him so they would *want* to worship Him and so they *would* worship Him in reverence and in awe."

There was silence again as the children thought about what Pastor Scotty had said. Then he continued, "The Bible is not just a story about people. The Bible is God's Word to His people to tell us about Him. Everything in the Bible teaches us who God is and what He did for us so that we can live in His presence. What happened to the Israelites is a picture of Jesus redeeming His church so that we can live with Him now and for all eternity. Look at the seven things God said that He would do for the Israelites. This is a picture of what Jesus did for us."

The kids were astonished. Finally Daniel spoke. "Jesus brought us out from under the yoke of Satan. He frees us and redeems us."

Mac continued, "And He takes us as His own people. He is our God."

"But what about the land?" asked Susie. "Is He going to give us some land?"

"Think about it." Pastor Scotty smiled.

Suddenly Mary jumped up. "It's heaven! He'll take us to heaven!"

Pastor Scotty had his serious look on his face. "When you know all of this, what does it make you want to do?"

Several voices answered, "Worship Him with reverence and awe."

LET'S TALK

Whom did Pharaoh think the Israelites belonged to?

Whom did they really belong to?

What did God want the Israelites to be free to do?

What is something we learn about God in this story?

What is something we should do because He redeems us?

What are the seven things you discovered about Jesus in this story?

CHAPTER FOURTEEN

An Awful Adventure

COVENANT PRIVILEGE AND RESPONSIBILITY: WORSHIP

Therefore, since we are receiving a kingdom that cannot be shaken, let us be thankful, and so worship God acceptably with reverence and awe.
(Hebrews 12:28 NIV)

"What do you wanna do today?" asked Caleb.

"I don't know. What do *you* wanna do?" replied Angus.

The boys were bored. "I want to do something new and adventurous! Not the same old stuff we always do!" Caleb declared.

The boys sat on the steps of Angus's house and thought for a while. "I've got it!" Angus announced suddenly. "Let's go check out the new neighborhood through the woods! There has to be adventure over there."

Caleb looked at him quizzically. "But . . . we'd have to cross the creek to get there."

The creek was a problem. Both boys' parents had forbidden them to cross it. It was a small creek, but the middle was surprisingly deep, and someone had reported seeing a snake in that area. Angus and Caleb continued to think about the situation. Finally Angus spoke. "My parents told me not to get *in* the creek."

"Mine too," Caleb agreed.

"But," Angus said with a grin on his face, "they never said anything about flying *over* the creek!"

Caleb was all ears.

"Follow me," called Angus. The boys ran to the garage, and Angus got two big bungee cords. Then the two explorers headed for the creek.

"Now explain this to me again," requested Caleb as they walked.

Angus began, "We're going to find two big trees at the edge of the creek that are about ten feet apart. We'll tie one end of one cord to one of the trees and one end of the other bungee cord to the other tree. Then we'll tie the bungee cords together."

Caleb nodded. "So it'll be like one big rubber band tied between two trees?"

"Exactly!" replied Angus. "Then we'll get in the middle and hold the bungee cord at our backs near our waists and back up as far as we can to stretch the bungee cord as much as possible," Angus explained.

"Oh! I get it!" exclaimed Caleb. "Then it will slingshot us right *over* to the other side of the creek—and we'll never get *in* the creek!"

Angus was quite proud of his idea. "And we never disobey our parents," he concluded.

The boys got to the creek, quickly found two trees, hooked up the bungee cords, and attached the two cords together. They took their place in the center of the cords and held the cords tightly across their backs. Then they backed up to stretch the cord. When it was as tight as they could get it, Caleb looked at Angus. "Are you sure this is a good idea?"

Angus was much too excited to listen. "When I say, 'Blast off,' lift your feet, and we'll fly right over to the other side."

Both boys took a deep breath. "BLAST OFF!" Angus yelled.

The boys lifted their feet, but the "blast off" was not quite what they had expected. The cord threw them immediately to the ground. In their sheer terror and confusion, neither boy let go of the cord. They were quickly dragged over the creek bank with such force that they plunged into the water. Fortunately, the water was only about waist deep. They slowly regained their sense of balance and stood up. Suddenly they remembered something important.

"SNAKES!" they screamed.

Caleb and Angus scrambled out of the creek and up the bank. They fell to the ground, unable to move another inch. Finally Angus said, "Every part of me hurts."

They sat up and surveyed their situation. They were filthy, their clothes were torn, and they had scrapes and cuts that were bleeding.

"We're a mess," moaned Caleb.

"Our parents are going to be so mad," muttered Angus.

The boys sat in silence. "I think I can move now," groaned Angus as he slowly stood up.

"That was the worst experience of my life," Caleb grunted.

The boys started the long walk home. The more they walked, the madder Caleb got. "This is all your fault," he blurted.

"No, it's not!" Angus protested. The boys argued until they came to the corner where Caleb turned and went to his house.

When Angus's mother saw him, she was horrified. While she bandaged his wounds, he told her what had happened. "Am I in trouble?" he asked as she tucked him in his bed.

"Oh, yes, but we'll talk about that later."

"I'm so mad at Caleb for blaming me for this mess," Angus pouted.

When Pastor Scotty got home, he sat on Angus's bed. He had a hard time hiding a chuckle as Angus told him about the awful adventure. Pastor Scotty told Angus what his punishment would be and then told him to get ready for dinner.

Angus was fuming. He thought to himself, *Caleb should have stopped me. I'll bet he's telling his parents it was my fault. He probably won't even get punished.*

At dinner Pastor Scotty told his family about his afternoon. "I finished working on my sermon and then spent time praying that God will prepare our covenant family to worship Him tomorrow. I kept thinking about Matthew 5:23-24, so I prayed that for our church."

"What do those verses say?" asked Susie.

Pastor Scotty reached for his Bible, opened it, and read, "'So if you are offering your gift at the altar and there remember that your brother has something against you, leave your gift there before the altar and go. First be reconciled to your brother, and then come and offer your gift.'"

"What does that mean?" asked Susie.

"It means that God does not want His children to be mad at each other. If we don't love each other, it will affect our worship of Him. So He tells us to be reconciled to our brother before we go to worship."

Angus was listening. The Holy Spirit softened his heart, and he realized that his anger was wrong. He also realized that the whole episode was his idea, and he couldn't blame Caleb for what happened. And he knew that he had no time to waste. Tomorrow was Sunday. "Dad," he asked, "will you take me to Caleb's house so we can be reconbiled?"

Pastor Scotty chuckled. "It's reconciled. It means to fix a friendship."

"I was hoping that's what it means." Angus grinned.

———◼———

LET'S TALK

What was the awful adventure?

Why did Angus and Caleb argue?

What does Matthew 5:23-24 tell us to do?

What happened to Angus when his dad explained Matthew 5:23-24?

What did Angus do?

CHAPTER FIFTEEN

The Neighborhood Dilemma

COVENANT PRIVILEGE AND RESPONSIBILITY: WORSHIP

*Therefore, since we are receiving a kingdom that cannot be shaken, let us be
thankful, and so worship God acceptably with reverence and awe.*
(Hebrews 12:28 NIV)

"Mom," called Angus, "all the kids are going to Jimmy's house. May I go?"

"Angus, we've discussed this a thousand times, and the answer is still no."

"But, Mom," Angus begged.

"You know the rule," she stated. The rule was that any of the neighborhood children could play at their house, but Angus and Susie were not allowed to freely roam in and out of other homes. None of the families on their street attended church. The parents often left the children home alone. Angus's parents did not like the language and the television programs allowed in other homes.

Angus went back outside. Jimmy and the other boys were waiting for him. "Hey, are you gonna come?"

"I can't," answered Angus, "but you can come to *my house* if you'd like."

"Oh, that would be fun," Jimmy said sarcastically as they headed over to his house.

Angus turned and slowly walked home. Later that afternoon the boys gathered to play football in the vacant lot on the corner. Angus ran down to join them.

"You really missed it," said Greg. "Jimmy's older brother got a new video game. His mom wasn't home, and he let us play it. It's the coolest game ever!"

All during the football game, Angus sulked. Why did his parents have to be so strict?

When the boys sat down to rest, one of them asked, "Why didn't you come to Jimmy's?"

"My mom wouldn't let me," answered Angus.

"Your mom wouldn't let you!" he teased. "She treats you like a baby."

Then it started. The boys were cruel. "Angus is a baby." "Do you want us to get you a bottle?" "Mama's little boy can't play with the big boys."

Finally Angus had had enough. "I wanna go play that video game," he announced.

"Let's go!" exclaimed Jimmy.

As they hurried to Jimmy's house, the other boys described the game. It sounded scary and violent. They were using terrible language that Angus had never heard before. He felt as if his brain were going to explode. Mixed in with the boys' words and laughter he kept thinking, *Worship God acceptably with reverence and awe.* His heart was pounding as they walked up the steps. He stopped and turned to the other boys. "Wait a minute! I'm not a baby, but I don't want to play this game, and I don't want to disobey my parents."

"You think you're so good because you're a preacher's kid," Greg sneered.

"I know I'm not good, but God is good. I don't want to dishonor Him," replied Angus. He turned and walked away as the boys continued to laugh and call him names. When he reached home, he went straight to his thinking place. After a while, his mom joined him.

"Do you want to tell me about it?" she asked.

Angus told her what had happened. She gave a huge sigh of relief. "I was afraid you had gone to Jimmy's and played the game. When you went to play ball, I started praying for you. I know those boys try to tempt you. I prayed that the Holy Spirit would remind you of Scripture verses and give you courage and protect you." Tears rolled down her cheeks.

Angus gave her a hug. "Thanks for praying for me, Mom. The Lord answered your prayers."

That night at dinner the family discussed the neighborhood dilemma. "I wish we could build a huge wall around our house and never have to see them," said Susie.

"I wish we lived on the same street with Caleb and Daniel and Mac," said Angus.

"I've thought the same things," admitted their mom. "But God put us on this street. This is the place where He wants us to serve and honor Him."

Pastor Scotty shook his head. "This is a sticky situation. It makes me angry when people are mean to you, and I want to protect you. But your mom is right—this is where the Lord has put us. Every Sunday the people on our street see us leave for church. When we come home, they're gathered in each other's backyards having cookouts. We must pray that they will see that our worship makes a difference in how we live."

"What can we do, Dad?" asked Angus.

"We can pray for them. Let's make a list, and each night we'll pray for one family."

"Good idea!" exclaimed Angus.

"And we can pray for grace to love our neighbors," said their mom. "Let's ask the Lord to show us ways to bless those who persecute us."

Susie smiled. "So instead of building a wall, we'll be missionaries in our neighborhood."

"Touchdown!" said her parents.

LET'S TALK

When the boys made fun of Angus, what did he say he wanted to do?

What did Angus think about as they walked to Jimmy's house?

Who caused Angus to remember the Bible verse?

What did Angus do?

What did Angus's mom pray?

CHAPTER SIXTEEN

A Plowed Heart

■

COVENANT PRIVILEGE AND RESPONSIBILITY: WORSHIP

*Therefore, since we are receiving a kingdom that cannot be shaken, let us be
thankful, and so worship God acceptably with reverence and awe.*
(Hebrews 12:28 NIV)

"Caleb, you have a letter," said his mom as she looked through the mail.

Caleb ripped the letter open. "Yipeeee!" he cried. "Ben from my soccer team is having a birthday party, and I'm invited. It's at the new ice-skating rink."

"That's great, Caleb. You've wanted to go there. What's the date? I'll write it on the calendar."

Caleb scanned the invitation and gave her the information.

"Oh, Caleb," she said, "that's a Sunday. I'm so sorry."

"But, Mom, please let me go. It doesn't start until after church, and I'll be through in time for evening worship. Please, Mom . . . you know how much I've wanted to try ice skating."

"Caleb, you know that your dad and I have made commitments for our family about keeping the Sabbath. We're to honor the Sabbath not just when we go to church but the whole day. Our reading time after lunch, and then our rest time is part of our Sabbath rest."

Caleb thought about his mom's words. He did enjoy hearing his dad read *The Pilgrim's Progress*. His dad teased that he guessed he would probably read this classic to his children at least twenty times before they were grown. But then Caleb thought about ice skating. "But, Mom," he began.

"Caleb, this is already settled. Your dad and I must obey God rather than please you." She picked up her Bible and read, "'Above all you shall keep my Sabbaths, for this is a sign between me and you throughout your generations. . . . Six days shall work be done, but the seventh day is a Sabbath of solemn rest, holy to the LORD. . . . Therefore the people of Israel shall keep the Sabbath, observing the Sabbath throughout their generations, as a covenant forever'" (Exodus 31:13, 15-16).

"Yes, ma'am," he said gloomily. He walked outside and got on his bike. Maybe a ride would help him feel better.

"Hello, laddie," called Sir John.

Caleb looked up. Sir John was sitting on his porch. "Hi, Sir John. What are you doing?"

"I'm plowing my heart, laddie."

Caleb stopped. He couldn't help but grin at the old gentleman. No matter how gloomy he felt, Sir John always made him smile. Caleb put down his bike and joined Sir John. He decided to ask the obvious question, though he knew there would be a lesson tucked in the answer. "Why are you plowing your heart?"

"Because I must get it ready," replied Sir John.

"Ready for what?" asked Caleb.

"Why, laddie, today is Saturday. I must get my heart ready for the Sabbath, and I have a heap o' work to do."

"Sir John, why do you have to get your heart ready for the Sabbath?"

"Ah, laddie, my heart is full o' hard places. I must ask God to show me my sin and to give me grace to repent. So I pray through Psalm 51. And then I must prepare my heart to listen."

"Prepare your heart to listen?" asked Caleb.

"Why, of course, laddie. Do you think that Pastor Scotty is the only one who has to prepare for the Sabbath? He must prepare to preach, but we must prepare to listen. We don't want

God's Word to fall on hard hearts. We must plow our hearts so they will be like good soil. Then when we hear God's Word, we'll bring forth gospel fruit."

"What kind of fruit?"

"Gospel fruit—the fruit of the Spirit. Here, take my Bible and look up Galatians 5:22."

Caleb opened the Bible and read, "'But the fruit of the Spirit is love, joy, peace, patience, kindness, goodness, faithfulness, gentleness, self-control . . .'"

"You see, laddie, when God's Word is preached, His Holy Spirit works in our hearts. He gives us power to trust and obey the Word. I want my heart to be ready to receive God's Word. Then His fruit will grow in my life. But there's something else I need to do to get ready."

"You mean there's more?" Caleb grinned.

"Ah, yes, laddie. Turn to Hebrews 10:24-25."

Caleb read, "'Let us consider how to stir up one another to love and good works, not neglecting to meet together, as is the habit of some, but encouraging one another.'"

"One way I prepare my heart is to pray for the people in our church. I ask God to help me know if someone needs a special word of encouragement."

"Is there anything else I need to know about preparing my heart?"

"Ah, yes, and this is most important. I set my thoughts upon God so that I will worship Him with reverence and awe."

"How do you do that, Sir John?" asked Caleb.

"Usually I read and think about one of the psalms. Today I'm meditating on Psalm 111."

"Thanks, Sir John. I think I had better go home and start plowing!"

Caleb's mom was sitting on the couch polishing her nails. He plopped down beside her. "Hi, Mom," he said sheepishly. "I'm sorry I was mad at you about the birthday party. I'm glad you and Dad honor the Sabbath and that you're teaching us about the Sabbath."

He watched as his mom put her polish down and began shaking her hands to dry her nails. "Your nails look good, but is your heart plowed?" he asked.

She gave him a puzzled look. "Have you been talking to Sir John?" she asked.

"How did you know?"

She smiled. "I can tell."

Caleb continued, "He said that we need to plow our hearts so we'll be prepared for the Sabbath. I've never thought about getting prepared before, but he's right."

"He's right a surprising amount of the time," she laughed.

Caleb kicked his shoes off. "I guess if we're going to do anything well, we need to get prepared. We have to get our 'game faces' on."

"Did Sir John say that?"

"No, I added that myself," admitted Caleb.

She reached over and gave him a great big hug, smearing her freshly polished nails. *Oh, well*, she thought to herself, *ruined fingernails but a plowed heart—it was worth it.*

LET'S TALK

Why couldn't Caleb go to the birthday party?

What was Sir John doing?

How did Sir John prepare his heart for the Sabbath?

If our hearts are like good soil, what kind of fruit will be produced?

How can you encourage others when you go to church?

PRAISE THE LORD!

[1]I will give thanks to the LORD with my whole heart,
 in the company of the upright, in the congregation.
[2]Great are the works of the LORD,
 studied by all who delight in them.
[3]Full of splendor and majesty is his work,
 and his righteousness endures forever.
[4]He has caused his wondrous works to be remembered;
 the LORD is gracious and merciful.
[5]He provides food for those who fear him;
 he remembers his covenant forever.
[6]He has shown his people the power of his works,
 in giving them the inheritance of the nations.
[7]The works of his hands are faithful and just;
 all his precepts are trustworthy;
[8]they are established forever and ever,
 to be performed with faithfulness and uprightness.
[9]He sent redemption to his people;
 he has commanded his covenant forever.
 Holy and awesome is his name!
[10]The fear of the LORD is the beginning of wisdom;
 all those who practice it have a good understanding.
 His praise endures forever!

CHAPTER SEVENTEEN

Glory Story—God Provides the Substitute for His People

EXODUS 7—12

■

A COVENANT PROMISE:

When I see the blood, I will pass over you. (Exodus 12:13)

A COVENANT PRIVILEGE AND RESPONSIBILITY: THANKFULNESS

Give thanks in all circumstances; for this is the will of God in Christ Jesus for you.
(1 Thessalonians 5:18)

The whistle blew, and immediately there was silence. "Covenant kids, why do you need to learn about your family history as Christians?" asked Pastor Scotty.

"Because our history is not about dead people," everyone shouted.

Then someone added, "It's about how God makes His people holy and blameless so we can live in His presence."

And someone else put in, "The people we talk about are living in God's presence right now. Their bodies have died, but their souls are with Jesus."

"First down! You're on the forty-yard line," called Pastor Scotty. "Let's keep this drive going. God called Moses to lead His people. What did He tell Moses to say to Pharaoh?"

A chorus of voices replied, "Let My people go."

"Another first down. You're on the thirty-yard line. Do you remember why God told Moses to tell Pharaoh to let the people go?"

"So they could worship Him," Mary offered.

"You're on the twenty. What did Pharaoh do?"

"He made things even harder for the people," replied Cassie.

"Ten-yard line—first and goal. What did God say He would do for His people?"

Mac jumped up excitedly. "God said He would bring them out from Egypt and free them and redeem them and be their God and take them to the land He promised."

Everyone shouted, "Touchdown!" Everyone, that is, except Mac. He was out of breath.

"Things were tough in Egypt," continued Pastor Scotty. "Over and over Pharaoh said the people could go, but each time he changed his mind. What did God do?"

"He made the water turn to blood—yuck," said Mary.

"He sent frogs and lice and flies," answered Caleb.

"The animals got sick, and the people had sores," added Susie.

"He sent hail and locusts and darkness," Daniel said.

Pastor Scotty continued, "Now let's hunker down and try to discover why God allowed all of this to happen. Mac, read Romans 9:17 to discover what God said about Pharaoh."

Mac read, "'For this very purpose I have raised you up, that I might show my power in you, and that my name might be proclaimed in all the earth.'"

Then Pastor Scotty turned to Caleb. "Would you read Exodus 10:1-2 to find out what God wanted the Israelites to know."

Caleb read, "'. . . that you may tell in the hearing of your son and of your grandson how I have dealt harshly with the Egyptians and what signs I have done among them, that you may know that I am the LORD.'"

Pastor Scotty explained, "God wanted His people to know that He is Lord. He is more powerful than the most powerful king on earth, and He is more powerful than the false gods the Egyptians worshiped. Mary, read Exodus 8:22-24 to find out what was happening to God's people during the plagues in Egypt."

Mary read, "'I will set apart the land of Goshen, where my people dwell, so that no swarms of flies shall be there, that you may know that I am the LORD. . . . I will put a division between my people and your people. . . . And the LORD did so.'"

Mary looked up from her Bible. "So God protected His people from the plagues. I guess they were beginning to understand how much He loved them."

"Yes!" exclaimed Pastor Scotty. "The people had lived under Pharaoh's power for a long time. They needed to know that Pharaoh was not in control. They needed to know about God's power and love so that they would worship Him with reverence and awe. Then God told Moses that the time had come for the final plague. He gave instructions to the Israelites."

Pastor Scotty opened his Bible and read Exodus 12:3-7, 12-13 (NIV):

> *"Tell the whole community of Israel that on the tenth day of this month each man is to take a lamb for his family. . . . The animals you choose must be year-old males without defect . . . all the people of the community of Israel must slaughter them at twilight. Then they are to take some of the blood and put it on the sides and tops of the doorframes of the houses where they eat the lambs. . . . On that same night I will pass through Egypt and strike down every firstborn—both men and animals—and I will bring judgment on all the gods of Egypt. I am the LORD. The blood will be a sign for you on the houses where you are; and when I see the blood, I will pass over you. No destructive plague will touch you when I strike Egypt."*

Pastor Scotty had his serious look again. "The Israelite dads did exactly what God said. They put the blood of the lambs on their doors. So God passed over those houses, and the oldest children did not die. God protected each home that had the blood on the door."

Everyone was quiet. Then Pastor Scotty asked, "When we're playing football, and one player takes another player's place, what is that player called?"

"A substitute," said all of the kids.

Pastor Scotty nodded. "The lamb was the substitute. The lamb died so that the oldest child would not have to die. If you had been the oldest child in an Israelite family, how would you have felt when you realized that you were spared because the lamb was sacrificed in your place?"

Mac spoke solemnly. "I would be sad that the lamb had to die, but I would be so thankful that I didn't. I think I understand, Pastor Scotty. Jesus is our substitute. He died in our place."

"Yes, Mac," replied Pastor Scotty. "Now turn to 1 Corinthians 5:7 and read it together."

Pages turned and voices recited, " 'For Christ, our Passover lamb, has been sacrificed.' "

Pastor Scotty didn't yell touchdown. He bowed his head and prayed. He thanked God that Jesus is the substitute and the Passover Lamb for His people.

■

LET'S TALK

What did God want the Israelites to learn from the plagues?

What did God tell the Israelite fathers to do?

What is a substitute?

What do you learn about Jesus in this story?

What should our attitude be to the fact that Jesus is our substitute?

CHAPTER EIGHTEEN

It's About Time!

■

COVENANT PRIVILEGE AND RESPONSIBILITY: THANKFULNESS

Give thanks in all circumstances; for this is the will of God in Christ Jesus for you.
(1 Thessalonians 5:18)

For months Pastor Scotty, Heather, Angus, and Susie prayed for the baby they wanted.

"It seems weird that someone in China will decide whether or not we can get a baby, when we can get a baby, and even which baby we get," remarked Angus.

"Is that really the way it works, Angus?" asked his dad.

Angus hit his head with the palm of his hand. "What am I thinking? Pharaoh thought he was in control, but all the time God was in control of when His people left Egypt. It's the same with our baby, isn't it?"

"Touchdown!" said his mom.

Angus had his thinking look on his face. "So I guess we should give thanks even while we wait because God is working everything out."

"He went for two and scored!" bellowed his dad.

A few weeks later Pastor Scotty bolted through the front door shouting everyone's name. Angus and Susie bounded down the steps. Heather ran from the kitchen.

"What's wrong?" they all asked at once.

Pastor Scotty was out of breath. "Telephone call . . . it's time . . . they have . . ." He stopped, and everyone shouted together, "*Our baby!*"

They all did the victory dance. They hugged, they laughed, and they cried, and they knelt together and thanked the Lord for their baby. Then Pastor Scotty told them everything he knew. "She's about nine months old. We leave in a few weeks to go get her. And listen to this—her Chinese name is Lian, which means 'graceful willow.'"

Angus, Susie, and Heather gasped. They had already decided to name their baby Grace. Heather was filled with wonder. "My great-grandmother Grace wanted to go to China as a missionary, but just before she was to leave, they stopped letting missionaries into the country. The rest of her life she prayed for the people in China, especially for the children. When she married and had children of her own, she prayed that her children and her children's children would love and serve Jesus and that they would love His people all over the world. I believe our baby from China is an answer to her prayers."

The next few weeks were a flurry of activity as they gathered the things they needed to take to China for their baby, bought airline tickets, set up a room for the baby, and asked Papa Sam and Mama Maggie to stay with Angus and Susie.

The day before they were to leave, Pastor Scotty saw Angus walk out to his tree house. *Uh-oh*, he thought. *He has on his thinking look*. Soon he followed Angus. "May I join you?" he asked.

"Sure, Dad."

"What's the problem?"

Angus put his head in his hands. "I've been thinking. What if I don't like the baby you bring back? What if she doesn't fit in our family? Or what if she doesn't like me?"

"Good questions," replied Pastor Scotty.

"Really?"

"Sure, but I have good answers." His dad grinned. "Angus, this is not just any baby. Before God created the world, He planned for us to adopt this exact baby. She belongs in our family. In some wonderful way God has arranged it all. There will be some hard adjustments. There were adjustments when you and Susie were born. But we'll love this baby because she belongs to us just as much as you belong to us."

Angus smiled. "Sometimes I forget how big and good God is," he admitted.

Inside, Susie sat on her parents' bed and watched her mom pack. Suddenly she was terrified. She began wringing her hands and chattering. "Mom, I've never been away from you for two weeks. You'll be so far away. Do you have to fly over the ocean? Will you be okay?"

Her mom stopped and sat on the bed beside Susie. "I'm sad about being away from you and Angus, and I have moments of panic when I wonder what we are doing. But then I think about the midwives who trusted and obeyed God and saved the Israelite babies. Let's pray that God will help us to trust Him. Get your Bible and let me show you a verse that comforts me."

Susie's mom read Psalm 139:9-10 (NIV). "'If I settle on the far side of the sea, even there your hand will guide me, your right hand will hold me fast.'"

Her mom explained, "Susie, I'll be on one side of the ocean, and you'll be on the other side, but God is in both places. He is with us both, and He will hold us tightly."

Susie began to calm down. "Thanks, Mom. I'm going to mark this verse so I can read it while you're gone. I guess we really can thank God in everything because He is with us both."

Her mom hugged Susie. "Oh, Susie, you're right. Thanks for reminding me to thank the Lord in everything. I suspect I'll need to remember that during the next two weeks."

LET'S TALK

Who decided which baby Pastor Scotty's family would get?

When did God make this adoption plan?

What was the baby's Chinese name?

What did the family plan to name her?

What did you learn about Angus's and Susie's great-great-grandmother?

CHAPTER NINETEEN

Sputters and Shrieks

■

COVENANT PRIVILEGE AND RESPONSIBILITY: THANKFULNESS

Give thanks in all circumstances; for this is the will of God in Christ Jesus for you.
(1 Thessalonians 5:18)

The day began early. The family piled into Papa Sam's huge van. "Are you sure you have everything?" Papa Sam asked Pastor Scotty.

"I hope so, Dad," Pastor Scotty answered.

"Your passports, airline tickets, traveler's checks?" Papa Sam continued.

"Yes, Dad." Pastor Scotty grinned. Papa Sam still thought of Pastor Scotty as his little boy.

"Don't worry about anything here," said Papa Sam. "I'll take good care of Angus and Susie. You take care of our new granddaughter and bring her home safely."

After they arrived at the airport, checked in, and said their good-byes, Papa Sam couldn't help slipping Pastor Scotty a little extra money. "Just in case you need it," he whispered. Pastor Scotty hugged his dad, and for a moment he felt like he was sixteen years old again.

"Don't forget, Mom," said Susie as they hugged. "Give thanks in all circumstances."

"You pray that I'll remember, and I'll pray for you too," whispered her mom.

On the way home, Papa Sam could tell that Angus and Susie were a bit sad. "Hey, kids, Mama Maggie and I have some special cupcakes for you when we get home!"

Mama Maggie gave him her what-in-the-world-are-you-talking-about look. She had not made cupcakes for the children, and she could tell by the gleam in Papa Sam's eyes that he was up to something. But the children had perked up; so she decided not to ruin the good mood. Maybe he had stopped by the bakery earlier.

Papa Sam continued, "These cupcakes are so terrific that I think we should have a party. We'll stop by and pick up Cassie, Caleb, Mary, Mac, and Daniel."

Now Mama Maggie was really giving him *the look*. She was a little worried about entertaining two kids, and now they were going to have seven! Papa Sam grinned. "Don't worry, Maggie. I'm ready."

All the kids loaded into the van, and Angus and Susie told everyone about their trip to the airport. When they got home, Papa Sam told them to go to the patio, and he would bring out the cupcakes. In a few minutes he joined them, carrying a huge tray. Mama Maggie was right behind him with cups and juice. The cupcakes looked so scrumptious that the children didn't notice the bewildered look on Mama Maggie's face or the mischievous grin on Papa Sam's face.

Papa Sam ceremoniously served the cupcakes. "Remember your manners, buckaroos," he instructed. "Don't begin until everyone has been served. . . . Now you may begin." He could barely control his laughter as the kids chomped down on his creations. In a few seconds there were sputters and shrieks of disgust.

"Yuck! This is terrible!"

Papa Sam erupted in laughter.

Mama Maggie looked at him. "You didn't get these from the bakery. You made them yourself!" She quickly poured juice for the kids. "I don't even want to know what you put in them! I'll never understand your sense of humor!" she exclaimed, though the kids could clearly see that she was having a hard time holding back her giggles.

"I can't believe you got us again," moaned Angus.

"Those were probably the worst-tasting cupcakes known to man," added Daniel.

"It was pretty funny though. I wish I had thought of it," said Mac.

"We now have a mission—to get even with Papa Sam!" Angus declared. They all laughed.

Papa Sam was sitting on a bench, holding his stomach and feeling sick from laughing so hard.

Mama Maggie sat down beside him. "Why do you play jokes on these kids?" she asked.

"Because it's so funny," he answered. Then in a moment of seriousness he added, "When people can laugh together, they will be able to cry together. This is a story these kids will remember."

"You know," she said, "they're going to get you back."

"I hope so," he said.

"Papa Sam," called Susie, who was still sputtering and spitting, "am I supposed to give thanks in this circumstance?"

Papa Sam exploded in laughter as Mama Maggie ran for more juice.

LET'S TALK

What did Susie tell her mom as she was leaving to go to China?

How did Papa Sam try to cheer the kids?

What did Angus say the kids' mission would be?

How does laughing together help us have stronger relationships with other people?

What does Romans 12:15 tell us to do?

CHAPTER TWENTY

The Lock-In

COVENANT PRIVILEGE AND RESPONSIBILITY: THANKFULNESS

Give thanks in all circumstances; for this is the will of God in Christ Jesus for you.
(1 Thessalonians 5:18)

"Do you really think this is a good idea?" Mama Maggie asked Papa Sam as they loaded sleeping bags into the van.

"Sure. Plus it's too late to back out now," he laughed.

"But I'm too old to sleep on the floor with little girls," she teasingly complained.

Papa Sam and Hunter, the youth director, had planned a lock-in at the church for the Covenant Kids Club. They knew the children would have a good time, and they thought it would help Angus and Susie to have something special to look forward to while their parents were in China. They were right. The week had passed much more quickly for Angus and Susie because of their excitement about the lock-in.

"We're ready!" called Angus and Susie as they came down the stairs with their sleeping bags and backpacks.

When the kids arrived at church, they gathered in the gym for games. Hunter had planned relay races and a pie-eating contest. The kids cheered as they competed against each other. Then Papa Sam announced that he had a new game, and he needed two volunteers. The kids looked at each other. They knew that with Papa Sam you needed to watch out for his jokes. Finally Mac and Angus reluctantly came forward.

Papa Sam had them stand about five feet apart. He handed Angus the end of a clear rubber tube. He handed the other end to Mac. "When I say, 'Go,' you are to blow in your end of the tube," he instructed. "We'll find out who has the strongest lungs."

Angus grinned. "You had me worried for a minute, but this is no big deal."

Mac agreed—until Papa Sam held up an egg, cracked it, and let the sticky mess drip into one end of the tube. Before the boys could protest, Papa Sam yelled, "Go!"

Angus and Mac started blowing. Neither wanted a face full of egg. The kids cheered. Papa Sam, anticipating what was soon to come, howled with laughter. Mac took his mouth off the tube to get a gulp of air and whosh! He had egg on his face! The gym erupted with glee as Angus and Mac fell to their knees laughing. Maggie came running with towels. She had learned from experience to have plenty of towels around when Papa Sam led games.

"Mac, you get the prize for being the best sport. Angus, you were a picture of determination!" exclaimed Papa Sam.

"The pizza's ready," called Mama Maggie. She looked at Papa Sam. "These kids are so wound up we'll never get them to sleep tonight."

"But they're having a good time, and they know that we love them," he laughed.

After everyone was stuffed with pizza, Hunter announced, "Papa Sam and Mama Maggie are going to tell us about their mission trip to Uganda. Then we'll make ice cream sundaes."

The kids cheered.

"Are you cheering for us or for the ice cream sundaes?" asked Papa Sam. Everyone laughed.

Papa Sam clicked on the PowerPoint and showed a map of Africa on the screen. "Here's Uganda," he said. "On this trip we flew a small plane into the country to deliver supplies to missionaries. We stayed in each village for a few days and then flew to get more supplies for another missionary."

Papa Sam showed pictures of children as Mama Maggie talked. "The people live in round, grass-thatched mud huts. They don't have running water. The children have to work hard. One of their chores is to get water from the village pump. They pump the water into jugs and then carry the jugs on their heads. The children also herd the goats, care for babies, and clean rice by picking out the stones and bugs."

Papa Sam laughed. "Mama Maggie didn't like the bugs."

Mama Maggie smiled. "Before we went, I was terrified that there would be roaches in our hut. I was sure I wouldn't be able to sleep. I prayed, and I slept like a baby and never saw a roach. However, at one of the meals they did serve us fried ants and grasshoppers! But they also had lots of fruit, for which I was very thankful."

Papa Sam showed pictures of people sitting on benches. "This is the church in one of the villages. Their houses and food are different from ours, but their love for Jesus is the same. Even though we could not understand their language, we could join them in praising the Lord. They're thankful that God sent a missionary to their village to tell them about Jesus. Mama Maggie and I are thankful for the joy of getting to know God's children all over the world."

Mama Maggie added, "And we're thankful for all of you who prayed for us. The Lord answered those prayers. Please continue to pray for God's church around the world."

Hunter thanked Papa Sam and Mama Maggie and then asked, "Who's ready for sundaes?"

"Do you think Papa Sam suspects anything?" Caleb whispered to Hunter.

"I don't think so," Hunter whispered.

When everyone had finished, Hunter went to the microphone. "I would like to have your attention. Papa Sam and Mama Maggie, the kids appreciate and love you so much that they have planned a special program in your honor!"

The children brought out two chairs covered in purple cloth. Hunter continued, "Please come and sit in these royal seats of honor." It was obvious that the secret had been guarded well. Papa Sam and Mama Maggie were stunned. Papa Sam tried to keep his pride in check, but he loved being the center of attention. He had a huge smile on his face as he sat in the special chair with the children gathered in front of him.

Cassie stepped forward, handed Mama Maggie a bouquet of flowers, and said, "We love you, and we appreciate you." Everyone clapped.

Daniel stepped forward and very seriously declared, "Papa Sam, we tried to think of something memorable to do for you because you are such a memorable fellow." Papa Sam was beaming. Daniel continued, "We tried to think of something that you will not soon forget . . ."

At that moment Hunter jumped from behind the chair and hit Papa Sam in the face with a cream pie! Papa Sam was startled. The kids exploded in laughter. "We gotcha!" they screamed with delight.

Papa Sam rubbed his finger over his face and then licked his finger. "Yummy! Thanks!"

Mama Maggie held her hands to both sides of her face in glee. "Well, at least he's thankful in all circumstances," she laughed.

LET'S TALK

Where did Papa Sam and Mama Maggie go on a mission trip?

What are some of the chores the children in Uganda do?

What are some of the things Papa Sam and Mama Maggie were thankful for?

What did the kids do to Papa Sam?

When is it wrong to throw a cream pie at someone?

CHAPTER TWENTY-ONE

Glory Story—
God Adopts His People

EXODUS 14—24

■

COVENANT PROMISE:

*I am the Lord your God, who brought you out of . . . the house of slavery.
(Exodus 20:2)*

COVENANT PRIVILEGE AND RESPONSIBILITY: LOVE

*You shall love the Lord your God with all your heart and with all your soul and
with all your mind. This is the great and first commandment. And a second is like
it: You shall love your neighbor as yourself. (Matthew 22:37-39)*

"Boy, I'm glad to be here—and I'm glad you're here," roared Papa Sam. "Pastor Scotty is still in China; so I get to tell you one of the most exciting stories in the Bible."

Angus grinned. "Papa Sam, you say that about every story in the Bible."

Papa Sam laughed. "You're probably right, but this lesson is packed with some of the most thrilling things you'll ever hear. Let's get started. After the tenth plague, Pharaoh said the Israelites could leave Egypt. But when they got to the Red Sea, they looked back and saw Pharaoh's army coming after them. He had changed his mind! They were trapped, and they were terrified. Mary, read Exodus 14:13-14."

Mary read, "'And Moses said to the people, "Fear not, stand firm, and see the salvation of the LORD, which he will work for you today. For the Egyptians whom you see today, you shall never see again. The LORD will fight for you."'"

Papa Sam continued, "I've been in some tight spots, but I've never been trapped like this.

The Israelites had nowhere to go. Then God parted the Red Sea, and they walked through on dry ground. When they were on the other side—CRASH!—the wall of water collapsed, and Pharaoh's army was never seen again. What a miracle of God's deliverance. Then the people traveled a few days into the wilderness, and they ran out of water. Soon they came to a place with water, but it was so bitter that they couldn't drink it. They complained, Moses prayed, and God showed him a tree and told him to throw it into the water. Immediately the water became sweet. Then God said, 'I am the LORD, your healer' (Exodus 15:26). What do you think God was teaching His people?"

The children were quiet. Papa Sam smiled. "Kids, life without Jesus is bitter. Because He died on the tree, on the cross, for our sin, He changes our bitterness into sweetness."

The children smiled back at Papa Sam, and he continued, "When the people arrived at Mount Sinai, Moses went up the mountain, and God said, 'This is what you are to tell the people.'" Papa Sam opened his Bible and read:

"You yourselves have seen what I did to the Egyptians, and how I bore you on eagles' wings and brought you to myself. Now therefore, if you will indeed obey my voice and keep my covenant, you shall be my treasured possession among all peoples, for all the earth is mine; and you shall be to me a kingdom of priests and a holy nation." (Exodus 19:4-6)

Papa Sam shook his head. "Kids, can you believe that? Everything in the world belongs to God because He made it. But He told the people that they would be His treasured possession. They would be a kingdom of priests and a holy nation. God was explaining to the people that He was adopting them as His own children."

"Adopting?" said one of the children. "That's like Pastor Scotty and Miss Heather."

"And it's like our memory verses from Ephesians," said Mac. He began reciting, and the other children joined him: "'For he chose us in him before the creation of the world to be holy and blameless in his sight. In love he predestined us to be adopted as his sons through Jesus Christ'" (Ephesians 1:4-5 NIV).

"You kids are great!" exclaimed Papa Sam. "Now whom did God adopt?"

Susie scrunched up her face. "Well, I guess he was talking about the people who were there, but I think He was talking about us too."

Papa Sam was so excited he was about to explode. "Yes! He was talking about all of His people who would ever live. He was talking about His church. Then God told Moses to consecrate the people. That means they were to be set apart for God. Then it happened." Papa Sam opened his Bible and read,

> *"On the morning of the third day there were thunders and lightnings and a thick cloud on the mountain and a very loud trumpet blast, so that all the people in the camp trembled. Then Moses brought the people out of the camp to meet God, and they took their stand at the foot of the mountain. Now Mount Sinai was wrapped in smoke because the LORD had descended on it in fire. . . . the whole mountain trembled greatly. And as the sound of the trumpet grew louder and louder, Moses spoke, and God answered him in thunder. The LORD came down on Mount Sinai, to the top of the mountain. And the LORD called Moses to the top of the mountain, and Moses went up." (Exodus 19:16-20)*

Papa Sam continued, "Then God gave the Israelites the Ten Commandments. Many years later someone asked Jesus which is the greatest of the commandments."

"What did Jesus say?" asked Susie.

"Let's find out," responded Papa Sam. "Look up Matthew 22:37-39."

Pages turned and Caleb said, "I've got it." He read, "'You shall love the Lord your God with all your heart and with all your soul and with all your mind. This is the great and first commandment. And a second is like it: You shall love your neighbor as yourself.'"

Papa Sam explained, "The Ten Commandments show us God's holy character. They teach us how to love God and each other. But none of us can keep these commandments. We break God's law. But Jesus kept every commandment. He was holy and blameless for us so that we can live in God's presence. What happened after God gave the Ten Commandments?"

No one knew.

Papa Sam opened his Bible. He was almost breathless as he read:

> *"Then Moses and Aaron, Nadab, and Abihu, and seventy of the elders of Israel went up, and they saw the God of Israel. There was under his feet as it were a pavement of sapphire stone, like the very heaven for clearness. And he did not lay his hand on the chief men of the people of Israel; they beheld God, and ate and drank." (Exodus 24:9-11)*

Everyone was quiet for a few seconds, and then Papa Sam continued, "We don't know exactly what they saw, but it was wonderful. They ate and drank with the holy, majestic King of the universe. They were His adopted children. And we're His adopted children. He is our God. He lives among us. We can't see Him, but He is with us. His Spirit actually lives within us to give us grace to love Him and to love each other."

LET'S TALK

When the water was bitter, what did God tell Moses to do?

What does this teach us about Jesus?

What does God call His people in Exodus 19:4-6?

What promises do you see in this story?

What did Jesus do for us? (Read Matthew 5:17; Galatians 3:13-14.)

What covenant privilege and responsibility do we have because Jesus kept the commandments and died for us?

THE TEN COMMANDMENTS

¹And God spoke all these words, saying,

²"I am the LORD your God, who brought you out of the land of Egypt, out of the house of slavery.

³"You shall have no other gods before me.

⁴"You shall not make for yourself a carved image, or any likeness of anything that is in heaven above, or that is in the earth beneath, or that is in the water under the earth. ⁵You shall not bow down to them or serve them, for I the LORD your God am a jealous God, visiting the iniquity of the fathers on the children to the third and the fourth generation of those who hate me, ⁶but showing steadfast love to thousands of those who love me and keep my commandments.

⁷"You shall not take the name of the LORD your God in vain, for the LORD will not hold him guiltless who takes his name in vain.

⁸"Remember the Sabbath day, to keep it holy. ⁹Six days you shall labor, and do all your work, ¹⁰but the seventh day is a Sabbath to the LORD your God. On it you shall not do any work, you, or your son, or your daughter, your male servant, or your female servant, or your livestock, or the sojourner who is within your gates. ¹¹For in six days the LORD made heaven and earth, the sea, and all that is in them, and rested the seventh day. Therefore the LORD blessed the Sabbath day and made it holy.

¹²"Honor your father and your mother, that your days may be long in the land that the LORD your God is giving you.

¹³"You shall not murder.

¹⁴"You shall not commit adultery.

¹⁵"You shall not steal.

¹⁶"You shall not bear false witness against your neighbor.

¹⁷"You shall not covet your neighbor's house; you shall not covet your neighbor's wife, or his male servant, or his female servant, or his ox, or his donkey, or anything that is your neighbor's."

Exodus 20:1-17

CHAPTER TWENTY-TWO

Surprise!

■

COVENANT PRIVILEGE AND RESPONSIBILITY: LOVE

You shall love the Lord your God with all your heart and with all your soul and with all your mind. This is the great and first commandment. And a second is like it: You shall love your neighbor as yourself. (Matthew 22:37-39)

"We're here," whispered Heather as the airplane touched down at the airport.

"I feel so far from home," remarked Pastor Scotty.

Heather opened her Bible and read Psalm 139:9-10: "If I settle on the far side of the sea, even there your hand will guide me, your right hand will hold me fast." They bowed their heads, and Pastor Scotty thanked the Lord that He was with them and that He would guide them.

There were nine other Christian couples in the group. They were all exhausted as they walked down the hall. "What do we do next?" asked one of the women.

"A guide from the adoption agency is supposed to meet us," answered another woman. "His name is William Wu, and they said he will take good care of us."

"I just hope he takes us to our hotel so we can get some sleep," moaned Heather.

They went to get their luggage. Pastor Scotty and Heather watched as everyone else claimed their bags. "I don't think ours made it," he finally muttered.

She groaned as she thought about being in a foreign country without even a toothbrush. Then she whispered, "Father, help me to give thanks in this circumstance." She smiled as she imagined Susie praying for her.

They met their guide. "Call me Willie," he said cheerfully. He helped them fill out the lost luggage forms, and then they joined the rest of their group already on the bus.

"Don't worry, we've all got extra clothes and supplies that we'll share with you," several people assured them.

"I even have extra toothbrushes. I'm a dentist," one of the men said.

Pastor Scotty and Heather felt comfort in the love of their Christian brothers and sisters.

The bus lurched forward and into a stream of traffic like none of them had ever seen. There were cars, trucks, motor scooters, bicycles, and taxis, all honking their horns as they barely missed bumping into each other.

The next day they did some sightseeing and shopping and took lots of photographs. They wanted Angus and Susie to know about the place where Grace was born, and they wanted pictures to show Grace when she was older. Finally the day arrived when they would get their baby. Their lost luggage arrived just before they left the hotel. "Thank You, Father!" exclaimed Heather. "We can take the presents we brought for Grace."

The bus was abuzz with excitement as everyone boarded for the ride to the orphanage. The group asked Pastor Scotty to lead them in prayer.

They arrived at the orphanage and were led to a large room. They waited . . . and waited. Finally a woman appeared with a toddler in her arms. "Mr. and Mrs. Joiner," she called.

A couple jumped up. "We're the Joiners," they said.

"Here's your baby." Everyone clapped.

Another woman came out and called someone else's name. Then Pastor Scotty and Heather were called. "Lian, meet your parents," said the woman.

Heather took the baby and held her close. Tears filled her eyes as she said softly, "You're beautiful. I love you. I love you." She handed the baby to Pastor Scotty.

He looked at her lovingly. "Graceful willow, welcome to our family. We have a new name for you. Your name is Grace for your great-great-grandmother who prayed for you. We pray that God will use you to praise His glorious grace."

On the bus ride back to the hotel, Heather and Pastor Scotty took turns holding Grace. They gave her a soft blanket to hold and the toys Susie and Angus had sent. "Grace seems sad," Heather whispered to Pastor Scotty.

"She'll be fine. She's just getting used to us," he replied.

The rest of that day and the next day Heather became increasingly worried about Grace. "I just know something is wrong," she insisted.

Everyone in the group knew that Heather was concerned. They all prayed for Grace. "I wonder if she had a special toy that was left at the orphanage," suggested one of the women.

"Maybe that's it!" exclaimed Pastor Scotty. "I'll get Willie Wu to make arrangements for us to go back and ask them."

"But you can't go back to the orphanage," Willie insisted. "You're all supposed to do more sightseeing. It would not be fair to the others."

"We don't care about sightseeing," called several voices. "We care about Grace. We want to go back to the orphanage."

Willie was bewildered. "Why do you all care so much about each other?" he asked.

One of the men smiled. "Because we're a family."

Willie was astonished. "Do you mean you are all one family?"

"We're all Christians," explained one of the men. "We're God's children, and so we're His family."

When the twenty adults and ten babies arrived at the orphanage, Willie explained the problem to the director. She whispered something to him. Everything was very secretive. Then she took him to her office. All the time Grace was frantically reaching her little arms toward the door and crying. Finally Willie came back. He seemed upset.

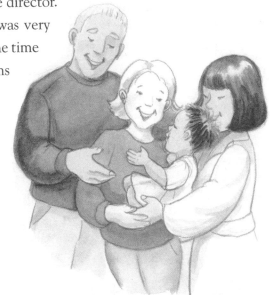

"Grace has a twin. Her name is Nianen," he said slowly.

"No wonder she's sad. She misses her sister," cried Heather.

Pastor Scotty was stunned. "A twin! . . . Then . . . we'll take her too!" he declared.

"You don't understand," continued Willie.

"The twin is not strong like Grace. She cannot be adopted. The director only told me this because she is worried about Nianen. Grace will be okay after a few days. You don't want a sick baby."

"Yes, we do! She's Grace's sister, and so she's our daughter. We love her," persisted Pastor Scotty.

"I'm sorry. It is impossible," replied Willie.

"With God all things are possible," declared Pastor Scotty.

All twenty adults immediately began praying. They asked the Lord to go before them and to work everything out.

Willie finally agreed to make the request. "Even if they agree to let the baby be adopted, it will be impossible to get all of the paperwork done before you are to leave," he pointed out.

"With God all things are possible," stated Pastor Scotty emphatically.

Willie shook his head. "But it's only a week before you leave."

LET'S TALK

What are some of the ways God used other people to show His love to Pastor Scotty and Heather?

Why was baby Grace unhappy?

What did Pastor Scotty and Heather want to do when they found out that Grace had a twin?

CHAPTER TWENTY-THREE

Joy!

———— ■ ————

COVENANT PRIVILEGE AND RESPONSIBILITY: LOVE

You shall love the Lord your God with all your heart and with all your soul and with all your mind. This is the great and first commandment. And a second is like it: You shall love your neighbor as yourself. (Matthew 22:37-39)

Grace was restless. Pastor Scotty paced back and forth in their room. "What can I do to get the agency to push this adoption through? Maybe I should fax our senator. Or maybe Dad could make some calls for us. Or maybe I should go to the adoption office early in the morning and refuse to leave until they tell me they will get the paperwork done."

He stopped pacing and looked at Heather. She was calmly rocking Grace. "You know what I'm doing, don't you?" He grinned.

She nodded.

"I'm trusting in chariots and horses and adoption agencies—and worst of all, I'm trusting in myself," he admitted. "I know what you're doing." He smiled. "You're praying for Grace and me."

He sat down beside her. They prayed, and then Pastor Scotty picked up his Bible. "I just remembered Moses' song after God parted the sea and His people walked across." He read,

> *"I will sing to the LORD, for He has triumphed gloriously; the horse and his rider he has thrown into the sea. The LORD is my strength and my song, and he has become my salvation; this is my God, and I will praise Him, My father's God, and I will exalt Him. . . . You have led in your steadfast love the people whom you have redeemed; you have guided them by your strength to your holy abode. . . . The LORD will reign forever and ever."*
> *(Exodus 15:1-2, 13, 18)*

They looked at Grace. She was sleeping soundly. "We need to trust our heavenly Father and rest in Him the way Grace is sleeping in your arms," whispered Pastor Scotty. "We are as helpless as she is, but our God's steadfast love and strength will guide us."

The next morning Willie Wu gave Pastor Scotty a list of places he would have to go to request permission to adopt Grace's twin. "You will have to hire another translator and a driver," he said. "I must take the rest of the group on the tour."

Immediately the group protested, "We want to go where they go. . . . We stick together," came several voices.

Heather hugged the women. "Thank you for showing us God's love," she said.

The next few days were an unforgettable adventure. They bounced along in the bus from office to office. Pastor Scotty and Heather stood in endless lines. Everyone helped care for Grace. At each place some people stayed on the bus and prayed while the others strolled through markets or parks with the children. On the fourth day Pastor Scotty and Heather ran out of the building, wildly waving some papers. "We can see Nianen . . . and we can bring her to the hotel."

Everyone cheered. "Do you mean you can adopt her?" they asked.

"It's not final yet, and they still say it can't be done before we leave, but they don't know our God!" announced Pastor Scotty triumphantly.

There was so much excitement that even Grace seemed happier. Pastor Scotty gave his camera to one of the men. "Be sure to get pictures of her face when she sees Nianen," he instructed.

"It's your face that I want to see," the man teased.

From the moment they arrived at the orphanage Grace whimpered and held out her arms. Willie gave the papers to the director, and they waited. Finally a woman came out holding a baby exactly like Grace, except that she was smaller. Both little girls squealed with delight. Cameras clicked, adults sobbed.

"Look at Grace. It's as if she has come alive," said one of the women.

"I've never seen such joy!" gasped one of the men.

Pastor Scotty and Heather looked at each other. "Joy!" they said at the same time, and they both knew that had to be her name.

The day before they were to return home, Willie Wu arrived at the hotel and announced to the group, "The impossible has happened." Everyone cheered.

Pastor Scotty said, "*Nianen* means mercy and thankfulness. Let us give thanks to God for His mercy to us."

Early the next morning the group left for the airport, and before they had time to think, twenty adults and eleven babies boarded an airplane, found their seats, and the plane took off. Pastor Scotty and Heather each had a baby in their lap. They looked at each other in astonishment.

"We . . . have *two* babies," Heather murmured.

"We didn't even have time to let Mom and Dad know," muttered Pastor Scotty.

"How are we going to take care of two babies?" asked Heather.

"How are we going to afford two more children?" asked Pastor Scotty.

"We'll trust the Lord," they both said together.

On the other side of the Pacific Ocean the anticipation was at a fever pitch.

"I don't know who I'll hug first," chattered Susie.

"I wonder what Grace looks like," said Angus.

"Just think—another granddaughter!" exclaimed Mama Maggie.

A lot of people from church arrived with food. Some tied yellow ribbons around the trees. Hunter and some of the teenage boys hung a big "Welcome Home" sign across the front of the house.

"It's time to leave," called Papa Sam. It looked like a parade going to the airport.

They gathered in the waiting area. Some were holding signs. The children had balloons. Angus, Susie, Papa Sam, and Mama Maggie stood at the front of the group.

"There they are!" someone yelled. Papa Sam took the baby from Heather's arms so she could hug Angus and Susie. At the same time Mama Maggie took the baby from Pastor Scotty. There was such a huge crowd and so much laughing and confusion that no one realized there were two babies.

Finally Susie shouted, "I want to see Grace."

"I have her," called Mama Maggie as she rushed to Susie.

At the same time Papa Sam called, "Here she is." He too rushed to Susie.

Instantly the noisy crowd was silent.

"We have a surprise," said Pastor Scotty as he grinned from ear to ear.

■

LET'S TALK

What did Pastor Scotty and Heather name Grace's twin?

Why did they name her Joy?

What did the people from the church do to welcome them home?

Everyone was surprised to see two babies. Do you think God was surprised?

When do you think God planned for Pastor Scotty and Heather to adopt two babies?

CHAPTER TWENTY-FOUR

They Don't Just Talk About Love

■

COVENANT PRIVILEGE AND RESPONSIBILITY: LOVE

You shall love the Lord your God with all your heart and with all your soul and with all your mind. This is the great and first commandment. And a second is like it: You shall love your neighbor as yourself. (Matthew 22:37-39)

"Two babies. . . . Pastor Scotty and Heather have two babies. . . . That means . . ."

Everyone scattered and scurried. They knew what had to be done, and they went to work!

"We have a crib in our attic," called someone, and off she went to get it.

"We have a high chair," offered another family.

"We need more diapers," said someone else.

The rest of the day there was a steady stream of people bringing baby supplies, helping care for the twins, and preparing food so Pastor Scotty and Heather could rest. Angus was in the front yard greeting all the visitors.

Jimmy watched from across the street. "Who are all those people coming to your house?" he called.

"They're from our church," answered Angus.

"Why are they bringing so much stuff?" continued Jimmy.

"Because they love us," replied Angus.

"Why do they love you?" questioned Jimmy.

"Because they love the Lord," Angus explained.

"Why?" asked a bewildered Jimmy.

Angus walked across the street and sat down beside Jimmy. "It's like this, Jimmy. We're all sinners—we break God's law. But Jesus came and kept God's law for us, and then He died to pay for our sin."

"Why would He die for us?" asked Jimmy.

"Because He loves us," declared Angus just as Jimmy's mom came outside.

"Hi, Angus," she greeted him. "I heard the news. How are the babies doing?"

"They're great," answered Angus.

A car stopped. Cassie, Caleb, and their parents got out with their arms loaded with bags of diapers. Angus jumped up and ran across the street to meet them.

Jimmy looked at his mom. "He sure talks a lot about love."

She smiled. "It seems to me that those people don't just talk about love."

That night everyone left, and the family sat down to a meal that had been prepared for them. Angus and Susie wanted to hear every detail about Grace and Joy. "They look just alike!" exclaimed Angus.

"But Joy is smaller," said Susie.

Their mom and dad explained that the people at the orphanage had said that Joy was not healthy. "Joy doesn't crawl yet, but Grace crawls everywhere. We'll take both girls to the doctor so they can be checked."

After dinner the family had their devotion time. Grace and Joy were a little wiggly, but they seemed to enjoy hearing Pastor Scotty read. Then Angus and Susie played with the little girls.

"Look at our happy little family," sighed Heather.

"You mean our happy big family," laughed Pastor Scotty.

When it was time for the girls to go to bed, everyone gave them big hugs. Pastor Scotty and Angus pushed the two cribs together so the girls could see each other. They all stood around the cribs and sang a song, and then Pastor Scotty prayed.

The next day Susie went with her mother to take the twins to the doctor. He examined the girls thoroughly. Finally he said, "Joy weighs less than Grace. She does not seem to have as much energy, and her eyes are not as bright, but I find nothing wrong with her. We need to keep watching her. I would like to see her again in two weeks."

Two weeks later they returned to the doctor. "Joy is eating everything we give her, and she's crawling," reported Heather.

The doctor watched the twins, and he watched Susie laughing and playing with them. He weighed Joy, and he tickled her toes. Her little eyes danced with delight. "I thought so," he said with a smile. "I don't think there's anything wrong with this little girl except that she was starved for love. She needed to be held and rocked. She needed to hear happy voices. She needed to be loved. Your family has given her love, and she's thriving now."

At dinner that night Susie and her mom told about the visit to the doctor. "I didn't know love would make a baby grow!" exclaimed Angus.

"Without love we shrivel up," said his mom.

Pastor Scotty nodded. "I think our whole family is thriving, even though we have had to make some big changes, because we're in a church that has loved us so well. God has used His family to show us His love."

He picked up his Bible and read,

> See what kind of love the Father has given to us, that we should be called children of God. . . . Beloved, let us love one another, for love is from God, and whoever loves has been born of God and knows God. Anyone who does not love does not know God, because God is love. In this the love of God was made manifest among us, that God sent his only Son into the world, so that we might live through him. . . . Beloved, if God so loved us, we also ought to love one another. (1 John 3:1; 4:7-9, 11)

"You know," mused Susie, "this makes me want to love others so they will thrive just like Joy."

LET'S TALK

Did the people from the church just talk about love?

What are some of the things the people did to show their love?

Why did they do these things?

Why was Joy not as strong and healthy as Grace?

What made her improve?

CHAPTER TWENTY-FIVE

Glory Story—God Is Good

EXODUS 33—34

■

A COVENANT PROMISE:

My presence will go with you, and I will give you rest. . . . I will make all my goodness pass before you. (Exodus 33:14, 19)

A COVENANT PRIVILEGE AND RESPONSIBILITY: GOODNESS

The fruit of the Spirit is . . . goodness. . . . (Galatians 5:22)

Pastor Scotty blew his whistle. "I'm sure glad to be here," he laughed. "I missed you while we were in China. Are you ready to learn more about our family history?"

"Yes, sir!" shouted the children.

"Why do you want to learn about our history?" questioned Pastor Scotty.

The kids answered together, "Because our history is not about dead people."

Daniel said, "It's about how God makes His people blameless so we can live in His presence."

Someone else added, "The people we talk about are living in God's presence right now. Their bodies have died, but their souls are with Jesus."

Pastor Scotty laughed. "It's good to be home. Now let's find out what happened after God gave the Israelites the Ten Commandments. While Moses was on the mountain, the Israelites mumbled and grumbled to Aaron, 'Where is Moses? We don't know what has happened to him. Make us gods to go before us.'"

Mary was shocked. "What did Aaron do?"

"He made a golden calf, and the people worshiped it," answered Pastor Scotty.

Now Mary was horrified. "What did God do?"

"Kids, open your Bibles to Exodus 32:35 and see if you can find the answer."

In a flash Angus declared, "The Lord struck the people with a plague."

"Touchdown!" said Pastor Scotty. "Then God told Moses to take the people to the land He had promised to give them, *but* He would not go with them because they were stiff-necked" (Exodus 33:3).

"What does stiff-necked mean?" asked Daniel.

"Good question." Pastor Scotty smiled. "It means they were stubborn and disobedient. Moses knew that the people did not deserve God's presence, but he knew that they needed it. Also he knew that God had promised that He would live among them. So Moses prayed, 'Consider that this nation is your people' (Exodus 33:13). Do you understand what Moses meant?"

Everyone was quiet, and then Mary said, "I think I do. Moses was thinking about God's covenant promise that they were His people and that He would not leave them."

Pastor Scotty bellowed, "Touchdown!" so loudly that the kids were sure the roof was going to cave in. "That's it! You've got it! Now see if you can find what God said."

When Cassie got excited, her voice became squeaky. "I see it! I see it!" she squeaked. "'My presence will go with you, and I will give you rest'" (Exodus 33:14).

Before Pastor Scotty could say a word, everyone yelled, "Touchdown!"

"You beat me," he laughed. "Then Moses prayed something else."

"I see it!" exclaimed Caleb. "'Please show me your glory'" (33:18).

Pastor Scotty continued, "Moses knew that he was going to have to lead thousands of stiff-necked people. He prayed to see God's glory so that he could reflect God's glory to the people. God had shown Moses some spectacular sights, but when Moses asked to see God's glory, what do you think God showed him?"

Everyone was quiet. Then Susie said, "I can't even imagine."

Pastor Scotty smiled. "It really is more than we can imagine. Susie, read Exodus 33:19."

Susie read: "'I will make all my goodness pass before you . . .'"

Pastor Scotty explained, "God told Moses that he could not see His face because the glory of it would be so powerful that Moses would die. But God said He would put Moses in a hollow place in the rock, and that He would pass by. The next morning that is what happened. Mac, read Exodus 34:6-7."

Mac read, "'The LORD passed before him and proclaimed, "The LORD, the LORD, a God merciful and gracious, slow to anger, and abounding in steadfast love and faithfulness, keeping steadfast love for thousands, forgiving iniquity and transgression and sin . . ."'"

Everyone was quiet. Pastor Scotty said softly, "Then Moses worshiped God. Kids, when Moses asked to see God's glory, what was the first thing God showed Moses?"

"That He is merciful," answered one of the children.

"Actually," said Pastor Scotty, "that was the second thing God showed Moses. But what was the first thing?"

Everyone looked at their Bibles. "Oh," said Daniel, "do you mean His name?"

"Yes!" said Pastor Scotty. "The name that God used here is the name that means He is faithful to His covenant people. He lives among us, and He keeps His promises to us. Then God described His goodness. It is merciful and gracious and slow to anger. It abounds in steadfast love and faithfulness and forgiveness. And do you know what happened? Angus, read verse 29."

Angus read, "'When Moses came down from Mount Sinai . . . Moses did not know that the skin of his face shone because he had been talking with God.'"

"Can you believe that?" exclaimed Pastor Scotty. "Moses' face was shining with glory! When we see God's glory, we will begin to reflect His goodness. That doesn't mean that our faces will shine. It means that our character will become more and more like God. Even when the people around us are stiff-necked, we will become more merciful and gracious. We'll be slow to anger. We'll abound in love. We'll forgive others."

"But, Pastor Scotty, how can we see God's glory? Where do we look?" asked Caleb.

"I was hoping someone would ask that." Pastor Scotty smiled. "Caleb, read John 1:14."

Caleb read, "'And the Word became flesh and dwelt among us, and we have seen his glory, glory as of the only Son from the Father, full of grace and truth.'" Caleb looked up from his Bible. "This is talking about Jesus, isn't it?"

"Yes, Caleb," said Pastor Scotty. "All of the Bible is about Jesus. When we read God's Word, we discover more and more about Him. And the more we know Him, the more we become like Him. He changes our hearts, and then His goodness shines through us. But there is something that keeps us from seeing and reflecting God's glory. What do you think it is?"

Mac replied, "I'm not sure, but my hunch is that it's our sin."

"Your hunch is exactly right," replied Pastor Scotty. "But our good and merciful God tells us that 'if we confess our sins, he is faithful and just to forgive us our sins and to cleanse us from all unrighteousness'" (1 John 1:9).

"I like this story," said Cassie.

LET'S TALK

Why did God say that He would not go with the people?

What does stiff-necked mean?

When Moses asked to see God's glory, what did God show him?

Where do we see God's glory?

What happens to us as we see more and more of God's glory in His Word?

What keeps us from seeing and reflecting God's glory?

CHAPTER TWENTY-SIX

It's Written on My Heart!

COVENANT PRIVILEGE AND RESPONSIBILITY: GOODNESS

The fruit of the Spirit is . . . goodness. . . . (Galatians 5:22)

Susie walked into her bedroom and let out a shriek. "Oh, no, not my box of beads!"

Her mom was right behind her. "Oh, Susie, I'm so sorry. I'll help you pick them up."

"I guess I'd better hide all my valuables," Susie sighed.

"At least put them high enough that the twins can't reach them," suggested Heather.

Joy and Grace had started toddling, and they were getting into everything. They had climbed on a chair and turned over Susie's craft box, and hundreds of colored beads were rolling everywhere. Some of the bead necklaces Susie had made were draped around Grace's neck. Grace screamed when Susie tried to take them off. Both girls had become very active and determined. Angus and Susie had been good sports, but Susie's patience was wearing thin.

"Joy and Grace are like the Israelites."

"How are they like the Israelites?" asked her mom.

"They're stiff-necked," replied Susie.

As Susie and her mom crawled around on their knees scooping up beads, Heather said, "The twins can be a handful, and I know it's frustrating when they get into your things. But do you remember what Moses prayed when the Israelites were stiff-necked?"

Susie thought for a minute. "He prayed that he would see God's glory."

"And what did God show him?"

Susie answered, "God showed Moses His goodness."

Her mom continued, "Susie, all of us are selfish and stubborn, but we're to love each other. We don't just love others when they're kind and loving. We're to love each other all the time. The way we can do this is to ask God to show us more of His goodness and to change our hearts so that we become more and more like Him. Then we begin showing His goodness to others. We'll be merciful, gracious, loving, and forgiving even when they're stiff-necked."

"But, Mom, what about when I'm so mad I don't want to be loving and forgiving?"

"Then you need to hurry to Jesus. Tell Him that you don't want to be good and that you can't be good without His grace. Ask Him to make you good."

"Mom, I'm not sure I can remember all of this. Will you write it down for me?"

Heather wrapped her arms around Susie and said, "I'll do better than that. I'll ask Jesus to write it on your heart so that you won't forget." They bowed their heads and prayed. Just as Heather said, "Amen," Grace and Joy toddled into the room. They both had something red smeared all over them. It looked like blood.

"Mom!" shrieked Susie.

Her mom laughed. "It's just jelly. They can be cleaned up."

"But what about the carpet?" moaned Susie.

"The carpet can be cleaned too." Her mom smiled. They each picked up a sticky, squirming baby and headed for the kitchen. Their mouths dropped open, and they froze in disbelief.

"This is a disaster!" exclaimed Susie.

"They were only out of our sight for a few minutes," said her mom.

Someone had left the jelly on the kitchen table after breakfast. It looked as if the twins had grabbed jelly by the handfuls and flung it everywhere. There was jelly on the refrigerator, on the cabinets, on the curtains, and . . .

"It's even on the ceiling!" groaned Susie. "How did they get jelly on the ceiling?"

"What are those speckled things?" asked a bewildered Heather.

"It's cereal!" Susie squealed. "They threw cereal, and it stuck to the jelly!"

"That's gross!" Heather had reached the edge of her patience. She was almost in tears. With each step she took, cereal crunched under her feet. She sat down on the kitchen floor and put her head in her hands.

"Mom, are you okay?" asked Susie.

"I don't know," Heather answered.

Susie bowed her head and closed her eyes. "Jesus, show us Your glory," she prayed. She opened her eyes and looked at her mom. "I remembered—it's written on my heart!"

Heather burst out laughing. "Oh, Susie, thank you! Now before we start this massive clean-up job, let's get a camera and take some pictures. One day this will make a great story to tell the twins."

———■———

LET'S TALK

How did Susie think Grace and Joy were like the Israelites?

Are we to love others when they are stiff-necked?

How can we love others?

What can we do when we don't want to love and forgive others?

What did Susie remember to pray when she saw the disaster in the kitchen?

CHAPTER TWENTY-SEVEN

Hurry, Angus—Pray!

■

COVENANT PRIVILEGE AND RESPONSIBILITY: GOODNESS

The fruit of the Spirit is . . . goodness. . . . (Galatians 5:22)

"Wait until Susie sees what I got," cried Angus as he jumped out of the car.

"Wait until Heather sees what I got," grinned Pastor Scotty.

Pastor Scotty and Angus had been to one of Pastor Scotty's favorite places—the home improvement store. When they arrived, they were surprised at what they saw in the parking lot. Clowns were selling tickets for a circus. There were even some ponies that kids could ride, and Angus had his picture taken on the pony. He was waving the picture as he ran into the house. Pastor Scotty was right behind him, waving tickets for the circus. *We stayed longer than we should have, but it was worth it*, he thought to himself. *I'll help Heather get everyone ready, and we can make it.* He felt like a kid. He had always loved the circus.

When Pastor Scotty and Angus walked into the kitchen, Pastor Scotty no longer felt like a little kid. "What a mess!" he moaned. Jelly and cereal were still everywhere.

"I didn't do it," Angus declared.

Pastor Scotty looked at his exhausted wife, who was scrubbing the wall while holding a squirming Grace in one arm. Susie was trying to keep Joy from stepping on the cereal.

"Honey, I'm so sorry," he said. "What happened?"

Heather explained as best she could. Pastor Scotty immediately went to work.

"But, Dad," protested Angus, "what about the circus?"

"What circus?" asked Susie.

"Dad bought tickets to take us all to the circus, but we have to hurry, or we'll be late."

"I'm sorry, Angus, but we'll have to forget about those tickets."

Heather offered, "You take Angus and Susie. I'll stay here and finish cleaning."

"Thanks, Mom," said Angus and Susie at the same time.

"Wait a minute. I'm not going to leave your mother with this mess. I should not have bought those tickets. It's harder for us to pick up and go now. I'm sorry, kids. Please forgive me."

Angus knew how much his dad loved his mom. He had watched him open doors for her, hold her hand, and bring her flowers. He understood, but he was really disappointed. "It's not your fault, Dad. It's the twins who cause so much trouble and spoil everything."

"Hurry, Angus—pray! Ask God to show you His glory," urged Susie.

"That sounds like good advice," laughed Pastor Scotty. "Let's stop pouting and complaining and get to work. Maybe we can make it to the circus. I'll clean the ceiling."

Angus was sure they couldn't get everything cleaned in time to go. He sulked as he slowly cleaned a cabinet. Then he realized that everyone else was working hard and fast. He started scrubbing faster. Maybe they really could finish in time to go.

Soon everything was clean. "We did it. We can still get to the circus on time."

"We'll go like we are— sticky hands and all," laughed Heather.

"No problem. They'll soon have cotton candy all over them," said Pastor Scotty.

As they drove to the circus, Angus was deep in thought. "Dad," he said, "I was really mad when I thought we couldn't go to the circus. I think I was stiff-necked. I'm sorry."

"Angus, it takes a lot of humility to admit when we're wrong. We're all stiff-necked, but

when we look to Jesus, He forgives us, and He shows us more of His goodness. Grace and Joy do cause trouble sometimes, but they're teaching us a lot about grace and joy."

"Yes, they are," laughed Angus as he listened to the two little girls squeal and giggle. Then he looked at Susie. She had been writing something. "What are you doing?" he asked.

She handed him her paper. "Help me with the last lines," she whispered.

He smiled as he read what she had written. "How about this?" He started writing.

After a few minutes Angus announced, "We have a poem." He read:

"To Grace and Joy, the best sisters of all:
You're sometimes clumsy, and you sometimes fall,
But you make us grin, and you make us smile,
Though we get mad at you every once in a while.
When you bug us, it makes us mad,
But when you're happy, we are glad.
We're so thankful that God gave you to us,
Though you keep things in quite a fuss.
The circus will be good, and the clowns will be funny,
But you're the ones who make our family happy and sunny."*

LET'S TALK

What did Pastor Scotty get for the family?

When Angus was upset with the twins, what did Susie tell him?

When Angus admitted that he was stiff-necked, what did his dad tell him?

*Adapted from a poem written by eleven-year-old Mary Kate for her younger sister Susie. Used by permission.

CHAPTER TWENTY-EIGHT

Cassie's Quandary

■

COVENANT PRIVILEGE AND RESPONSIBILITY: GOODNESS

The fruit of the Spirit is . . . goodness. . . . (Galatians 5:22)

"Hello, lassie," called Sir John.

Cassie looked up. "Oh . . . hi, Sir John."

"You seem to be in deep thought," said the old gentleman.

"Yes, sir, I'm in a quandary." She walked up to join Sir John on his porch. "Umm, what's that yummy smell?"

"Ah, Miss Jenny is making some of her famous apple pies. Would you like to go in and watch?"

"Yes, sir!"

Sir John smiled. *A little girl's quandary and a woman's apple pies are a good combination*, he thought to himself.

"Hi, Miss Jenny. Sir John said I could watch you."

"Hello, Cassie. How are you today?"

"Well, I'm in a quandary. That's a funny word, isn't it? I just learned it. But my quandary is not funny."

"Would you like to talk about it?"

"Actually I would," said Cassie as she climbed on a stool. "My quandary is about our memory verse."

"What's your memory verse?"

Cassie sounded pretty miserable as she recited, "'The fruit of the Spirit is . . . *goodness*.'"

"Cassie, that's a wonderful Bible verse. What's the problem?"

Cassie sighed. "I'm having a hard time being good."

"Would you like to tell me about it?"

"Well, Caleb makes me so mad. He laughed at me this morning when I tripped over my long nightgown. When I yelled at him for laughing at me, he said I was a bad sport. Then we both got in trouble for arguing. Sometimes my brother and my friends are like the Israelites—they're stiff-necked."

"There's a problem with your friends too?" asked Miss Jenny.

Cassie put her head in her hands. "A girl in my Sunday school class annoys me. She always wants to sit next to me, but then she's mean to me. She grabs things from me, and she marks on my paper."

"That *is* a problem," said Miss Jenny. "What do you do?"

"Well," said Cassie slowly, "I guess I'm stiff-necked too. I get mad and say mean things to her. I know I'm supposed to be good, but sometimes I just don't want to be good." She sighed again. "Miss Jenny, I want to please God, but I'm tired of trying to be good."

"Ah." Miss Jenny smiled. "There is an answer to your quandary." She picked up a bright, shiny apple. "Where do you think this apple came from?"

"Your apple tree," replied Cassie. Everyone on their street and at church knew about Miss Jenny's beautiful apple trees and her delicious apple pies.

"I did not make these apples. They are the fruit of the apple tree. Why do my trees have so many tasty apples?"

"Because you take such good care of them," answered Cassie. Everyone also knew that Miss Jenny worked hard to care for her apple trees.

"Cassie, goodness is the fruit of the Holy Spirit. I think that maybe you're trying to make the fruit yourself, and that will make you very tired. You're trying to *act* good rather than asking the Holy Spirit to change your heart so that you will *be* good."

Cassie pondered this while Miss Jenny took two steaming pies from the oven and put two more in.

"But why do I have such a hard time being good?" asked Cassie.

"Well, when my apple trees were first planted, they did not produce a big crop of beautiful apples. I had to water and fertilize the trees. At first I just got some hard, little apples. But the more I took care of the trees, the more fruit I got. The Holy Spirit lives in our hearts, but the Bible tells us things that we must do so that His fruit will grow in us. Read what Jesus tells us in John 15:4-5."

Cassie picked up Miss Jenny's Bible. "As the branch cannot bear fruit by itself, unless it abides in the vine, neither can you, unless you abide in me. . . . Whoever abides in me and I in him, he it is that bears much fruit, for apart from me you can do nothing."

Cassie looked up. "What does abide mean?"

"It means to remain with Him or to stay with Him. The Holy Spirit comes to stay with us, and we need to learn to stay with Him."

"How do I do that?" Cassie asked.

"God uses His Word to cause us to grow. When we read our Bibles, and pray, and go to church, God uses those things as fertilizer and water for our spiritual life. He causes us to grow in the grace and knowledge of Him, and more of His fruit grows in our lives. Jesus is with us all the time, and we can talk to Him all day long. Now read Matthew 3:8."

Cassie read, "'Bear fruit in keeping with repentance.'"

Miss Jenny smiled. "Sometimes apples look fine on the outside, but they're rotten on the inside. Good fruit will not grow in a heart that is rotten with sin. When we repent, God forgives us. Then good fruit will grow. The longer we let sin stay in our hearts, the more rotten it becomes. As soon as you feel annoyed, angry, or jealous, hurry to Jesus and ask Him to forgive you. Now read Hebrews 13:15-16."

Cassie read, "'. . . let us continually offer up a sacrifice of praise to God, that is, the fruit of lips that acknowledge his name. Do not neglect to do good and to share what you have, for such sacrifices are pleasing to God.'"

Miss Jenny explained, "When we recognize God's goodness and love and mercy, and we praise Him, we will become more like Him. When we think about all that He does for us, we will want to share His goodness with others."

"Miss Jenny, why are you making so many pies?"

Miss Jenny laughed. She loved the way children switch from one topic to another without missing a beat. "My trees have a lot of apples on them this year. I picked all of these this morning; so I decided to make apple pies for my friends. One of these is for your family."

"I thought so," said Cassie. "You're doing good and sharing with others. I think it's because you abide in Jesus."

Miss Jenny was startled. Cassie had not switched to another topic. She understood what Miss Jenny had been telling her. She was growing in the grace and knowledge of Jesus.

LET'S TALK

What was Cassie's quandary?

Who produces the fruit of goodness in our lives?

What are some things we can do so that the fruit of the Spirit will grow in our lives?

Why was Miss Jenny making so many pies?

CHAPTER TWENTY-NINE

Glory Story—God Is Merciful

EXODUS 25—31

■

A COVENANT PROMISE:

You in Your mercy have led forth the people whom You have redeemed; You have guided them in Your strength to Your holy habitation. (Exodus 15:13 NKJV)

A COVENANT PRIVILEGE AND RESPONSIBILITY: MERCY

He has shown you, O man, what is good; And what does the Lord require of you but to do justly, to love mercy, and to walk humbly with your God? (Micah 6:8 NKJV)

Pastor Scotty blew his whistle. "How many of you like to build things?" he asked.

All of the boys raised their hands.

"Dad and I designed and built a bookcase for my room," said Daniel.

"I've seen that bookcase, and it's really cool." Pastor Scotty grinned. "Who likes to sew?"

"I do," declared Mary. "Granny Grace is teaching Cassie and me to make doll clothes."

"Well, you kids would have enjoyed what God told the Israelites to do next," continued Pastor Scotty. "God told Moses to build a tabernacle. The word *tabernacle* means 'dwelling place.' The tabernacle would be God's dwelling place among the people. God told Moses every detail about the size and color and shape of everything in the tabernacle. They were to follow these instructions exactly because the tabernacle teaches us how to come to God. Everything in the tabernacle teaches us something about Jesus, because it is through Jesus that we can come to God."

Pastor Scotty drew a picture of the tabernacle as he talked. "The tabernacle was divided into three parts. First, there was the courtyard with the altar of burnt offering. What do you think they did at the altar?"

"Burned stuff!" called one of the children.

"That's right," Pastor Scotty chuckled. "They offered animals as sacrifices. The people could not approach God without a sacrifice for their sins. What does this teach us about Jesus?"

"I think I know," said Mary softly. "Jesus died as our sacrifice so that we can come to God."

"Does that make you think of a Bible verse?" asked Pastor Scotty.

Mary nodded. She began reciting 1 Corinthians 5:7, and all the children joined her: "'For Christ, our Passover lamb, has been sacrificed.'"

Pastor Scotty smiled. "Then there was the laver. This was like a big bowl, and it was filled with water. This is where the priests washed before they went into the tabernacle."

"Dad," exclaimed Susie, "does that teach us that Jesus washes away our sin?"

"Yes! Susie, read Ephesians 5:25-26."

Susie read: "'. . . Christ loved the church and gave himself up for her . . . having cleansed her by the washing of water with the word. . . .'"

"This is incredible," declared Daniel. "I never knew that the tabernacle tells us about Jesus."

Pastor Scotty was pumped! He loved seeing the children get excited about God's Word. "Now let me tell you what was inside the tabernacle. The front section was called the Holy Place. There were three pieces of furniture and a candlestick with seven candles."

"Oh, I know what that teaches," Cassie announced. "Jesus is the light of the world!"

Pastor Scotty nodded. "Next there was a table with bread. Mac, read John 6:35."

Mac read, "'Jesus said to them, "I am the bread of life; whoever comes to me shall not hunger, and whoever believes in me shall never thirst."'"

Pastor Scotty continued, "In front of the curtain was the altar of incense. When you burn incense, there's a sweet smell. The Bible says that prayers offered to God are like sweet fragrance going up to Him (Psalm 141:2). The Bible also tells us that Jesus is in heaven interceding, or praying, for us. Caleb, read Romans 8:34."

Caleb read, "'Christ Jesus is . . . at the right hand of God, who indeed is interceding for us.'"

"Jesus *prays* for *me*," said Cassie slowly. "That's wonderful. What's next, Pastor Scotty?"

"Now we come to the best part," he answered. "There was a beautiful curtain that sepa-

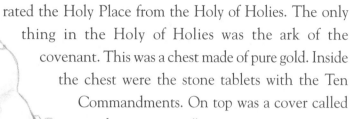

rated the Holy Place from the Holy of Holies. The only thing in the Holy of Holies was the ark of the covenant. This was a chest made of pure gold. Inside the chest were the stone tablets with the Ten Commandments. On top was a cover called the mercy seat."

Pastor Scotty closed his eyes. The children knew that he was praying, asking God to help them understand what he was going to tell them next. They waited.

"Kids, we cannot come to God by keeping the Ten Commandments because we can't keep them. We break God's Law every day. God is a just God, and His justice must be satisfied. Let me explain. Let's pretend someone robbed a bank, and he's caught. He's taken before a judge, and the judge says, 'Oh, that's okay. You broke the law, but I'm not going to punish you.' What would you think of that judge?"

"He's not a good judge," answered the children.

"He didn't do what's right," added Mac.

"Exactly," said Pastor Scotty. "But God is a just Judge. Sin must be punished, but the Law was covered with the mercy seat."

"Pastor Scotty, what's mercy?" asked Mary.

"Good question," replied Pastor Scotty. "Mercy means not getting what we deserve. We deserve to be punished for our sin, but our sin is covered with God's mercy because Jesus was punished for us. And God does more. He gives us His grace, His love, that we don't deserve."

Mary's face brightened. "So mercy is *not* getting what we deserve, and grace is *getting* what we *don't* deserve."

Pastor Scotty was speechless. He couldn't even yell touchdown. Finally he took a deep breath and said softly, "Kids, the mercy seat stands for the place where God meets with His people. When was God's justice fully satisfied, and where do we see God's mercy to His people?"

Everyone said, "Oh! At the cross!"

Pastor Scotty said, "Everything in the tabernacle showed how people could meet with God. All of this is a picture of what Jesus did so that we can be God's children. Now I'll tell you about one of the most spectacular things that has ever happened."

The children's eyes opened wide.

Pastor Scotty explained, "The moment Jesus died on the cross, the curtain between the Holy Place and the Holy of Holies ripped apart. Because of Jesus, God's people are not separated from Him. The Bible says that we can come boldly into His presence. We can talk to Him. He is our God, and we are His people. He is a God of mercy, and His mercy endures forever."

The children sat in stunned silence. After a few moments Caleb said, "That's awesome."

———■———

LET'S TALK

What does the tabernacle teach us?

Whom does everything in the tabernacle teach us about?

What does the candlestick with candles teach us about Jesus?

What was in the ark of the covenant?

What was on top of the ark?

What is mercy?

What is grace?

Oh, give thanks to the Lord, for He is good!
For His mercy endures forever.
(1 Chronicles 16:34 nkjv)

For He is good,
For His mercy endures forever.
(2 Chronicles 5:13 NKJV)

For He is good,
For His mercy endures forever toward Israel.
(Ezra 3:11 NKJV)

For the Lord is good;
His mercy is everlasting,
And His truth endures to all generations.
Psalm 100:5 (NKJV)

Praise the Lord!
Oh, give thanks to the Lord, for He is good!
For His mercy endures forever.
(Psalm 106:1 NKJV)

Praise the Lord of hosts,
For the Lord is good,
For His mercy endures forever.
(Jeremiah 33:11 NKJV)

CHAPTER THIRTY

Miss Kate

■

A COVENANT PRIVILEGE AND RESPONSIBILITY: MERCY

He has shown you, O man, what is good; And what does the Lord require of you but to do justly, to love mercy, and to walk humbly with your God? (Micah 6:8 NKJV)

"You look wonderful. Remember your manners," reminded Susie's mom. "Mama Maggie and Miss Kate don't go to restaurants with playgrounds and prizes in the meals."

Miss Kate was ninety years old. She was the oldest member of the church. Every week Mama Maggie took her to lunch, and then they went to the nursing home to visit. Susie had been invited to join them.

Susie kissed Grace and Joy good-bye. As her dad drove her to meet Mama Maggie, he asked, "What does the Lord require?"

"'To do justly, to love mercy, and to walk humbly with your God,'" Susie answered.

"Very good. Do you know what mercy is?"

"I've forgotten," replied Susie.

"Mercy means not getting what we deserve. It means goodness, kindness, and loyalty. Mercy is faithful, loving service to others. All through history God's people have shown mercy to the poor, the lonely, the sick, and the elderly."

"Dad, is that what I'm going to do with Mama Maggie today? We're going to visit the elderly."

Pastor Scotty nodded. "Yes, Susie, and I pray that you learn to love mercy just like Mama Maggie."

Mama Maggie and Susie picked up Miss Kate. "You look so pretty," said Susie. Miss Kate had on a lovely pink dress, and she smelled like roses.

"Well, ladies, I think we should go to the new tea room. I hear it's wonderful," announced Mama Maggie.

At the restaurant a nice lady greeted them and took them to a table. She smiled at Susie. "Would you like to look in our little girls' dress-up trunk?" Susie followed her. She gasped when she looked in the trunk. "You can put them on," said the lady. Susie returned to the table wearing lacy gloves, a feathery pink boa, a hat with roses, and a fancy purse. Mama Maggie and Miss Kate giggled as much as Susie.

After they ordered, Mama Maggie asked Miss Kate to tell Susie some stories about when she was a little girl. Miss Kate's eyes twinkled as she told about having five younger brothers and sisters and riding in a horse-drawn buggy to church. "I remember the first car I ever saw," laughed Miss Kate.

Susie was spellbound.

"My favorite memory is of my Saturdays with my grandmother. Saturday mornings she and my mother prepared food. In the afternoon Grandmother delivered the food to poor families. Mama couldn't go because she had so many children, but when I was just about your age, I began going with my grandmother. Sometimes we took soup to older people who were sick. Sometimes we visited young mothers with sick children. Wherever we went, Grandmother talked to them about Jesus. She read the Bible and prayed. People loved to see her. They said she was an angel of mercy. Soon I knew that I wanted to be just like my grandmother."

Miss Kate had a faraway look in her eyes as she continued, "God lit a fire in my heart to help other people. I knew that I had found my ministry."

They were all quiet for a few minutes, and then Mama Maggie asked, "Miss Kate, what was your favorite Bible verse when you were a little girl."

Miss Kate smiled. "As Grandmother and I walked from house to house, she recited verses to me. They are still some of my favorites." She closed her eyes and recited, "'For He delivers the needy when he calls, the poor and him who has no helper. He has pity on the weak and the needy' (Psalm 72:12-13). 'You, LORD, have helped me and comforted me' (Psalm 86:17)."

Miss Kate opened her eyes and looked at Susie. "Grandmother told me that God created woman to be a helper. She explained that redeemed women can be what God created us to be because God is our Helper. She told me that we can be merciful to others because God is merciful to us."

Susie waited while Miss Kate slowly took a sip of tea.

"The winter I was fifteen, there was a lot of sickness. We did not have the medicines that are available today. My grandmother died, and two weeks later my mother died. Suddenly I had to be a mother to my five younger brothers and sisters. The youngest was just six months old. At first I was sad that I could not visit the sick and helpless. I thought I had lost my ministry as well as my mother and grandmother, but one day I remembered what my grandmother had said. Every Saturday I would ask her who we were going to help that day. She always said the same thing: 'Whoever needs our help.' I realized that the ones who needed my help were my little brothers and sisters. They were the ministry the Lord had given me." Miss Kate smiled triumphantly. "And God answered my prayers for them. He gave them hearts to know and love and serve Him."

"Do you have any other favorite Bible verses, Miss Kate?" asked Susie.

"I was hoping you would ask. When my grandmother was dying, she said Psalm 100:5 to me. I think about it every day." Miss Kate closed her eyes. "'The LORD is good; His mercy is everlasting, and His truth endures to all generations'" (NKJV).

Mama Maggie's eyes shone with tears. "Thank you, Miss Kate," she said softly. "Well, ladies, the food and the fellowship were wonderful. I think it's time for us to go."

When they arrived at the nursing home, Miss Kate went to one room, and Mama Maggie and Susie went to another. The afternoon was over too quickly for Susie. When she walked into her house, her mom had just put the twins down for a nap. "Tell me all about it," she urged.

Susie, the chatterbox, told her every detail about the tea room and about Miss Kate. Then she told about the nursing home. "Mama Maggie wrote letters for Miss Jane, and I put pretty stickers on the letters. We visited Mr. Thompson, and he told me about his wife. Mama Maggie said that even though his wife is no longer living, it makes him happy to talk about her. Mama Maggie said I should ask the Lord to give me a husband whose love for me will last as long as he lives. Then we visited Miss Barbara and Miss Carol. They have pictures of missionaries all over their room. Mama Maggie painted their fingernails and read to them, and then we prayed for some of the missionaries."

Susie got up and started upstairs to change her clothes. She turned back to her mother. "Mom, I think God lit a fire in my heart. I think I have found my ministry."

Her mom smiled, and she thought to herself, *She sounds a lot like Mama Maggie and Miss Kate—and that's a good thing.*

LET'S TALK

What was Miss Kate's favorite Bible verse?

Who is our Helper?

What was Miss Kate's prayer for her younger brothers and sisters?

What did Susie and Mama Maggie do at the nursing home?

CHAPTER THIRTY-ONE

The Reformation Day Party

◼

A COVENANT PRIVILEGE AND RESPONSIBILITY: MERCY

He has shown you, O man, what is good; And what does the Lord require of you but to do justly, to love mercy, and to walk humbly with your God?
(Micah 6:8 NKJV)

"What are you gonna be tonight?" Jimmy asked Angus. It was October 31.

"Moses! I've got the Ten Commandments and everything," answered Angus.

"Moses? Isn't he a Bible guy? That's not scary," Jimmy scoffed.

"It's not supposed to be scary," replied Angus. "We don't celebrate Halloween. That's about ghosts and goblins and scary things. We celebrate Reformation Day."

"What's that?" asked Jimmy.

"It's the day Martin Luther nailed his ninety-five theses on a church door and started the Protestant Reformation. We're having a Reformation Party at church tonight."

"You talk about church way too much," Jimmy complained.

"You would too if you went to my church. It's a lot of fun."

"Fun? Church isn't fun."

Angus told Jimmy about the party. "There'll be a dunking booth. If you hit the target with a baseball, Hunter, our youth pastor, will drop into the water tank. There'll be a pin-the-theses on the church door game, and we'll get prizes."

"And the party is *tonight?*" Jimmy was beginning to sound interested.

"Yeah." Angus had a big smile on his face as he thought about the fun. Then it hit him! "Jimmy, do you wanna come with me?"

"I sure do! But do you get any candy?"

"Tons!" Angus beamed.

When they arrived at church, everyone made quite a to-do about Susie, Grace, and Joy. They wore the beautiful dresses Pastor Scotty and Heather had brought from China. There were a lot of visitors, and the kids made them all feel welcome.

"Cool costume," Caleb said to Jimmy. Jimmy was dressed as an army man. Caleb was a football player.

Jimmy looked at Daniel. "That's a great costume, but what are you supposed to be?"

Daniel was dressed as a monk. "I'm the star of the show."

Jimmy looked confused.

"You'll understand when you hear Dad's story," explained Angus as the boys filed out to play the games.

Jimmy's favorite game was throwing pies at clowns as they stuck their heads through holes in a screen. Angus liked the duck shoot game where they shot at rubber ducks with water pistols.

"Who are all these adults?" asked Jimmy as they walked to the back of the church.

"They're people in our church," explained Angus.

"They sure seem to like kids," Jimmy remarked.

"They love us. We're their covenant kids," replied Angus. Then his jaw dropped in amazement. "Wow! This is better than last year!" he exclaimed as he saw the huge blow-up obstacle course. "Come on," he called, and the boys raced through the maze.

After the hay ride everyone gathered for story time. Pastor Scotty began, "Tonight we have a special guest who will give a firsthand account of the

Protestant Reformation. Our visitor comes to us from the year 1517. Ladies and gentlemen, please welcome Martin Luther!"

Everyone clapped. "Is that Hunter?" Caleb whispered to Angus.

"Yeah. I think he's having a bad hair day. Maybe it's because he got dunked so many times." They laughed. Hunter had on a Martin Luther-style wig.

Jimmy looked at Daniel. "He's dressed just like you," he whispered.

"I told you I was the star." Daniel grinned.

Hunter began, "I was born in Germany. My parents wanted me to become a lawyer, but God had other plans. My parents taught me about God, but they didn't understand about His grace and mercy. I never thought that God loved me. I thought I had to be good enough to earn my way to heaven. When I was a teenager, my parents sent me to a school in another town. And that's when it happened . . ."

Hunter spoke softly. Everyone listened. They didn't want to miss a word. "One day I went home to visit my parents. As I walked through the woods, there was a terrible storm—lightning, thunder, wind, rain, and hail! I was sure I was going to die! Lightning struck a tree, and it crashed to the ground!"

Hunter clapped his hands, and the kids jumped.

"I fell on my face and called out to God. I promised that if He would save me, I would forsake the world and become a monk. Suddenly the storm ended. My teachers and friends tried to convince me not to go to the monastery, but I was sure that becoming a monk would make me good enough to earn my way to heaven. At the monastery, there was a large Bible chained to a stand in the dining hall. I stood for hours reading that Bible. When I became a priest, the other monks gave me a Bible as a present. I could not believe that I had my very own Bible."

Hunter paused. He wanted the children to think about the privilege of having their own Bibles. He continued, "I was invited to teach at the University of Wittenberg, and later I was sent to Rome with a message for the pope. In Rome there was a staircase that people believed Jesus climbed on the way to His crucifixion. People thought that if you climbed those stairs, it would make you more holy. I had become a monk, but I still felt the guilt of my sin. I was desperate to find forgiveness; so I decided that I would not just climb the stairs."

Hunter dropped to his knees. "I decided to crawl on my hands and knees and to kiss each step as I recited many prayers. But as I climbed, the Holy Spirit reminded me of a Bible verse, Romans 1:17: 'The just shall live by faith'" (NKJV).

Hunter jumped up. "Finally I understood! I could never be good enough to earn salvation. It was by grace through faith in Jesus Christ that I could be forgiven. When I got back to Wittenberg, I taught my students that we're saved by grace and not by good works. I began to be troubled because the leaders in the church were more interested in raising money than in teaching the gospel. The priests sold indulgences, a piece of paper that said your sins were forgiven. I was furious! They were selling forgiveness like you sell a loaf of bread! I protested by writing ninety-five theses, or arguments. I nailed these to the church door, which was like the community bulletin board. I didn't mean to stir up trouble. I just wanted to let the people know what the Bible says. Soon news of this spread all over Germany."

Hunter shook his head. "The church leaders were enraged! They ordered me to stand trial. They wanted me to admit that I was wrong. I asked if I could have until the next day to give them my answer. I prayed all night. I knew they could sentence me to be executed. The next afternoon I stood before them again."

Hunter paused. Jimmy was sitting on the edge of his seat. "What did he do?" he whispered to Angus.

Hunter stood up straight. "This is what I told them: 'I cannot deny what I have written and taught, for I believe it is the truth. My conscience is bound by the Word of God. I cannot act against my conscience. Here I stand; I cannot do otherwise. So help me God.'"

Hunter turned and walked out. Everyone clapped. Pastor Scotty finished the story. "Martin Luther was condemned by the church, but his friend Prince Frederick arranged for him to be 'kidnapped' and taken to an isolated castle. There Luther translated the New Testament into German so the people could have God's Word in their own language. Later he returned to Wittenberg and spent the rest of his life serving God and the people. Now Mr. Luther wants to introduce you to a special lady."

Hunter came back, escorting a woman in a long dress. "It's Mama Maggie," whispered the children.

Hunter began, "This is Ursula Cotta. When my parents sent me to school, they did not have money to give me for food. The boys from the school walked the streets singing, hoping someone would invite us in for a meal. One day I was hungry and discouraged. No one had given me anything to eat. I was sure I would have to leave school and work in the mines with my father. Then a door opened, and dear Ursula invited me in. She fed me, and later she and her kind husband invited me to live with them. I began to do better in my studies. This woman's kindness and mercy were used by the Lord to prepare me for the work He had for me to do."

Mama Maggie smiled. "I had no idea when I fed that scrawny boy that I was helping the Father of the Reformation."

Everyone clapped. Jimmy looked at Daniel. "Your costume is really cool," he said grinning.

"Candy time!" shouted Pastor Scotty. "The adults are ready to give you candy. Why do they give you treats?"

"Because they love us," the kids shouted as they scrambled to get in line.

LET'S TALK

What did Angus's church celebrate on October 31?

Who is the Father of the Reformation?

What did Martin Luther do on October 31, 1517?

What are some things you learned about Martin Luther?

What did Ursula Cotta do?

CHAPTER THIRTY-TWO

A Right Fight

COVENANT PRIVILEGE AND RESPONSIBILITY: MERCY

He has shown you, O man, what is good; And what does the Lord require of you but to do justly, to love mercy, and to walk humbly with your God?
(Micah 6:8 NKJV)

Cassie ran her tongue across her front gum as she looked in the mirror. *I sure look different,* she thought. She had lost both of her front teeth the night before. Excitedly she hurried to the kitchen to greet her family. "Good morning, Mom. Where'th Caleb?" She looked startled. "Why do I thound tho funny?"

"Because you need front teeth to pronounce some words."

Just then Caleb came through the door. "Good morning, Cassie. How are your teeth . . . or rather your lack of teeth?" he joked.

"Okay, I gueth. But I talk kinda funny," she answered.

Caleb could tell that Cassie was a bit self-conscious. "You sound fine," he said.

That afternoon Cassie went to show Sir John and Miss Jenny that she had lost her teeth. Later Caleb was riding his bike. He looked up and saw Cassie walking home faster than usual. Then he saw that she was crying, and noticed a bunch of boys a ways behind her. He ran to meet her.

"Cassie, what's wrong?"

"Thoth boys . . . they won't thop making fun of the way I talk," sobbed Cassie.

Caleb had seen the boys before. They lived several blocks away.

"So you talk funny, and you're a crybaby," one of the boys yelled.

Caleb didn't know what to do. "Come on, Cassie. Let's go home."

One of the boys ran up and stepped between Cassie and Caleb. "Who are you?"

"I'm her brother. Leave her alone and let her by," Caleb demanded.

"I won't leave her alone. What are you gonna do about it?"

Cassie was crying harder. Caleb could feel blood rushing to his head. "Lord, help me!" he prayed silently. Then he said calmly, "I don't want any trouble. Just move and let her by."

The boy lunged at Caleb, pushed him, and then swung his fist at him. Somehow Caleb dodged the punch. Before even thinking about it, Caleb threw a punch of his own. It landed right on the boy's nose. The boy fell on the ground, holding his nose and screaming just as Caleb's dad pulled into the driveway and got out of his car. The boy jumped up and ran. The other boys were already out of sight.

"Caleb, what's going on?" called his dad as he ran to them.

Caleb was trying to comfort Cassie. He looked at his dad. "I'm sorry. I know it's wrong to fight, but they were being mean to Cassie. She was scared, and they wouldn't leave her alone."

"Let's go inside, kids."

As they walked inside, Cassie told her dad what had happened. "Caleb protected me, Dad."

Caleb plopped down on the couch and put his head in his hands. "Dad, I feel terrible. I wanted to do the right thing. I asked the Lord to help me. But I ended up fighting."

"Caleb, I know you're confused about this. It's hard to know when it's right to fight. We should do everything we can to avoid arguments and fighting, and it sounds as if you did. The other boy threw the first punch. It's acting justly to protect those who cannot protect themselves. Son, you did a good and right thing to defend your sister."

"Really?" asked a very relieved Caleb.

"Really. But you do have a responsibility to those boys. How can you show them mercy?"

"I guess I could pray for them," suggested Caleb.

"You're exactly right, and as you pray for them, the Lord will fill you with more of His goodness. You also need to ask the Lord to give you grace to forgive the boys."

"But they haven't asked for forgiveness," said Caleb.

"It doesn't matter. We forgive others because God has shown us mercy and forgiven us. Ask the Lord to take away any anger or desire for revenge and to give you His love for the boys."

Caleb's dad reached for a book. "Caleb, in 1917 during the First World War, President Theodore Roosevelt was asked to write a message to be put in the front of New Testaments that would be given to American soldiers. He quoted Micah 6:8 and commented:

"Do justice; and therefore fight valiantly against those that stand for the reign of Moloch and Beelzebub on this earth. Love mercy; treat your enemies well; treat every woman as if she were your sister; care for the little children; and be tender with the old and helpless. Walk humbly; you will do so if you study the life and teaching of the Savior, walking in His steps."

Caleb and his dad prayed together. Then Caleb said, "I think I'll go check on Cassie."

"Before you go," said his dad, "I have a question. Where did you learn how to throw a punch like that?"

"I have no idea," grinned Caleb.

LET'S TALK

Why was Cassie talking funny?

What did Caleb do when he saw her crying?

Who started the fight?

How did Caleb try to avoid the fight?

How could Caleb show mercy to the boy?

Why should Caleb forgive the boy?

What president wrote comments on Micah 6:8 in the front of New Testaments for soldiers?

CHAPTER THIRTY-THREE

Glory Story—God Dwells Among His People

EXODUS 40

■

A COVENANT PROMISE:

And they shall know that I am the Lord their God, who brought them out of the land of Egypt that I might dwell among them. (Exodus 29:46)

A COVENANT PRIVILEGE AND RESPONSIBILITY: UNITY

I have given them the glory that you gave me, that they may be one as we are one: I in them and you in me. May they be brought to complete unity to let the world know that you sent me and have loved them even as you have loved me. (John 17:22-23 niv)

The whistle blew. "Covenant kids, you are part of God's covenant family. Do you want to know your family history?" shouted Pastor Scotty.

"Yes, sir!" answered the kids.

"Why?" asked Pastor Scotty.

"Because our history is not about dead people," called one of the kids.

"Our history is about people who are living in God's presence right now," added someone else.

"Our history is about how God makes His people holy and blameless so that we can live in His presence," answered another.

Then everyone yelled, "Touchdown!" while Pastor Scotty did his silly dance.

The kids were excited to see Hunter, the youth pastor, and several of the teenagers. Pastor

Scotty explained, "We're going to learn more about the tabernacle, and they're going to help us. When Moses and the people finished building the tabernacle, something wonderful happened." Pastor Scotty opened his Bible and read, "'So Moses finished the work. Then the cloud covered the tent of meeting, and the glory of the LORD filled the tabernacle'" (Exodus 40:33-34).

The children were speechless. Cassie asked, "What did it look like?"

Pastor Scotty smiled. "We don't know, but it was magnificent. The cloud reminded the people of God's promise to live among them. But where do you think they put the tabernacle? Mary, read Numbers 2:1-2."

Mary read, "'The LORD spoke to Moses and Aaron, saying, "The people of Israel shall camp each by his own standard, with the banners of their fathers' houses. They shall camp facing the tent of meeting on every side."'"

Pastor Scotty continued, "The tabernacle was to be in the middle with everyone camped around it. The Israelites were divided into twelve tribes." He divided the kids into twelve groups, assigned each group to a teenager, and gave each teenager a big sheet of paper with the name of a tribe written on it. "Now decorate your banners," he instructed.

While everyone worked on the banners, Pastor Scotty put a table in the middle of the room and draped a cloth over it. When the banners were finished, he told the kids to pretend that the table was the tabernacle. He explained which direction was north. Then he told the teenagers to read Numbers 2 and figure out where their tribes should be. After a lot of scurrying, everyone was in place.

The tribes of Dan, Asher, and Naphtali were on the north. The tribes of Judah, Issachar, and Zebulun were on the east. The tribes of Ephraim, Manasseh, and Benjamin were on the west. And the tribes of Reuben, Simeon, and Gad were on the south.

"Which way are you supposed to face?" asked Pastor Scotty.

There was a lot more scurrying as everyone turned toward the tabernacle.

"Now, kids, pretend you are an Israelite. What do you see?"

"I see the glory cloud," said Susie dramatically.

"Me too!" exclaimed the others.

Pastor Scotty continued, "This is a beautiful picture of the church, God's covenant family. The thing that made the Israelites different from all the other people in the world was that God lived among them. They saw His glory. They belonged to Him. What do you think this teaches us?"

Caleb thought about Moses asking to see God's glory and God showing Moses His goodness. He said, "I think it teaches us that we're all supposed to look at God's glory and then show His goodness to each other."

"Touchdown!" Pastor Scotty grinned.

Cassie continued, "And I think it teaches me that my family is not just Mom and Dad and Caleb. It's everyone in our church."

"Right, Cassie," replied Pastor Scotty. "And it's even bigger than that. Our covenant family is all of God's children all over the world. And it's even bigger than that. Who else do you think it is?"

Cassie pondered this for a moment. Her eyes sparkled as she said, "It's also all of the people who are already in heaven."

Pastor Scotty was about to burst with excitement. "Yes! We're connected to God's other adopted children all over the world, and we're connected to those who have lived before us and those who will live after us. There's something else I want you to understand. Look at your banners. What do you notice about them?"

Everyone looked. "They're all different," said Mac thoughtfully.

"And what do you think that teaches us?"

Mac's eyes lit up. "We're all different, but we're part of God's family."

The kids thought Pastor Scotty was going to explode. They laughed as he did his victory dance and kept yelling, "Touchdown!" When he finally calmed down, Daniel asked, "Pastor Scotty, where is the tabernacle now?"

"Good question! The word *tabernacle* means "dwelling place." Daniel, read John 1:14."

Daniel read, "'And the Word became flesh and dwelt among us, and we have seen his glory, glory as of the only Son from the Father, full of grace and truth.'"

Pastor Scotty explained, "The Word is Jesus. He became a man and dwelt, or tabernacled, among us. Jesus is the tabernacle. He is the meeting place between God and His people. But listen to this! Daniel, read 2 Corinthians 6:16."

Daniel read, "'. . . we are the temple of the living God; as God said, "I will make my dwelling among them and walk among them, and I will be their God, and they shall be my people."'"

Daniel looked up. "Does this mean what I think it means?" he asked.

"Yep," smiled Pastor Scotty. "God's dwelling place is in the hearts of His covenant people. We are His tabernacle. And listen to what Jesus prayed for us. Mary, read John 17:22-23."

Mary read, "'I have given them the glory that you gave me, that they may be one as we are one. . . . May they be brought to complete unity to let the world know that you sent me and have loved them even as you have loved me'" (NIV).

Mac looked up from his Bible. "Does this mean that Jesus has given *us* His glory?"

Pastor Scotty nodded. "And why has He given us His glory?" he asked.

The children all looked at the verse. Angus answered, "So that we will be one—so there will be unity among us." He looked at his dad. "What's unity, Dad?"

"Unity is the opposite of divided. It means that we are joined together in our desire to glorify God. It means that we love one another because God loves us. Kids, what will happen when there is unity among us?"

Everyone looked at their Bibles. Cassie's voice was filled with wonder as she said, "The world will know that God sent Jesus and that God loves us." Then she said what everyone was thinking. "Pastor Scotty, this is bigger than my brain can hold."

"You're right, Cassie, but your heart can hold it."

———■———

LET'S TALK

What happened when the tabernacle was completed?

Where was the tabernacle to be placed?

What were the people to face?

Where is the tabernacle now?

What does unity mean?

CHAPTER THIRTY-FOUR

The Responsibilities

■

COVENANT PRIVILEGE AND RESPONSIBILITY: UNITY

I have given them the glory that you gave me, that they may be one as we are one: I in them and you in me. May they be brought to complete unity to let the world know that you sent me and have loved them even as you have loved me.
(John 17:22-23 NIV)

"Is everyone packed and ready? Mimi and Pop will be here in a few minutes."

"Yes, sir," called Cassie and Caleb.

Soon the big motor home pulled into the driveway. They loaded luggage and coolers of food, and they were off.

"I can't wait to see all the cousins," said Cassie as she sat at the table and played a game of Old Maid with her mom and Mimi. Caleb and his dad sat up front with Pop.

"So Shannon is joining the church," Caleb said in his most grown-up voice. "I've been thinking of doing that myself."

Shannon was his oldest cousin. The whole family was going to be with her when she made her public statement of faith and became a member of the church. Pop, Mimi, and all the uncles and aunts had decided that this was a big event and that the family should be there to celebrate it together.

Pop questioned, "Why do you want to join the church, Caleb?"

"Well, I love Jesus . . . and at our church you can take Communion after you've joined the church."

"And why do you want to take Communion?" asked his dad.

"Uhh . . . I don't know." Caleb could tell by the looks on the men's faces that they were not thrilled with his answers. "You probably think I'm too young to join the church," he said.

His dad laughed. "Yep, but this is a good time for us to talk about it. Caleb, you belong to our church family because you're our child. You enjoy the privileges of being a part of God's covenant family. The people in our church love you, they pray for you, and they teach you God's Word. You've trusted Jesus to be your Savior, but that doesn't mean that you're ready to take on the responsibilities of church membership."

"I'm pretty mature. I think I could handle the responsibilities," said Caleb.

A Volkswagen Beetle passed by. "Punch buggie!" Caleb yelled and punched his dad in the arm playfully.

His dad laughed. "Yeah, Caleb, you're real mature! Seriously, son, think about it like this. You have some responsibilities in our family, but you don't have the major responsibilities of protecting and providing for our family. The same is true in God's family. Shannon is a teenager. She's been a Christian since she was a little girl, but now it's time for her to take her covenant responsibilities in God's family."

The motor home came to a stop. The door of the coach flew open, and Cassie and Caleb bounded out. Their feet barely hit the ground before they were surrounded by the cousins. James and Jason grabbed Caleb and started wrestling on the ground. "Cassie!" Kellie and Laurin squealed as the girls hugged. Pop and Mimi were holding babies. Everyone was laughing and talking at the same time.

"I'm so glad you're here!" exclaimed Shannon. "Come on, kids, I've planned a great scavenger hunt for you."

Uncle Dean and Aunt Kathryn led the adults inside.

After dinner Pop gathered everyone together. Uncle Dean escorted Shannon to a chair in front.

Pop began, "Shannon, you're our oldest grandchild. We're grateful for the legacy of grace that God has given you. He gave you a mom and dad who have taught you about Him. He gave you a church family who has helped your parents teach you. He gave you a heart to trust Him when you were just a little girl. You've grown in the grace and knowledge of Jesus, and now you're ready to make a public statement of your faith before your church family and to take on the covenant responsibilities of church membership."

Pop looked at the younger cousins sitting on the floor. "Your parents and uncles and aunts and Mimi and I prayerfully look forward to the time when each of you will be ready to do what Shannon is doing."

He looked back at Shannon. "We have gifts for you. We pray that these gifts will remind you of the blessed privilege and responsibility of being a member of God's covenant family."

Shannon's mom and dad gave her the first gift. It was a beautifully framed print of some Bible verses. "Shannon," said Uncle Dean, "these 'One Anothering' verses tell us some of the responsibilities of being a part of God's family. Our prayer is that you will love God's church and that you will reflect your redemption by sharing your gifts and graces with His people."

The uncles and aunts gave Shannon a Bible with her name and the date printed on the cover.

Mimi's eyes shone with tears as she handed Shannon a book.

Shannon gasped, "It's an old copy of *Stepping Heavenward.**"

"Look inside," said Mimi excitedly. "I found it at an antique store. It was given to a young girl by her grandmother in 1887. Shannon, this book has helped generations of women to step heavenward as they journeyed through this life. I pray that it will do the same for you."

Then Pop presented Shannon with his gift. It was a pearl necklace. "This belonged to my mother," he said tenderly. "Jesus said that the kingdom of God is like a pearl of great price. Her favorite Bible verse was 'Seek first the kingdom of God and His righteousness . . .' (Matthew 6:33). That's what she did, and I pray that you will too."

*Stepping Heavenward, by Elisabeth Prentiss, has been reprinted by several publishers.

"There's one more gift," said Caleb. "Shannon, the cousins made a bookmark for your Bible. It has the cousins' covenant on one side and all of our names on the other side."

"What a perfect way to conclude this wonderful time," observed Pop. "Cousins, gather around Shannon and say your cousin covenant together."

"Photo-op!" called Mimi. "Get the cameras."

After a few moments of confusion, the cousins were in place. Cameras clicked as they recited together, "'And they entered into a covenant to seek the LORD, the God of their fathers, with all their heart and with all their soul' (2 Chronicles 15:12)."

LET'S TALK

What was Shannon going to do?

What are some of the privileges of being a part of God's family?

What are some of the responsibilities of being a part of God's family?

What did Pop give Shannon?

What did the cousins give Shannon?

ONE ANOTHERING

Love one another: just as I have loved you.
(John 13:34)

Live in such harmony with one another, in accord with Christ Jesus, that together
you may with one voice glorify the God and Father of our Lord Jesus Christ.
(Romans 15:5-6)

Welcome one another as Christ has welcomed you,
for the glory of God.
(Romans 15:7)

Through love serve one another.
(Galatians 5:13)

Be kind to one another, tenderhearted, forgiving one another, as God in Christ
forgave you.
(Ephesians 4:32)

Encourage one another and build one another up,
just as you are doing. (1 Thessalonians 5:11)

Stir up one another to love and good works.
(Hebrews 10:24)

Pray for one another.
(James 5:16)

Love one another earnestly from a pure heart.
(1 Peter 1:22)

Show hospitality to one another without grumbling.
(1 Peter 4:9)

Beloved, let us love one another, for love is from God.
(1 John 4:7)

CHAPTER THIRTY-FIVE

This Is Big . . . *Really* Big!

COVENANT PRIVILEGE AND RESPONSIBILITY: UNITY

I have given them the glory that you gave me, that they may be one as we are one: I in them and you in me. May they be brought to complete unity to let the world know that you sent me and have loved them even as you have loved me.
(John 17:22-23 NIV)

The next morning was frenzied pandemonium. The adults were panting when they straggled out of the house to get in cars to go to church. "Caleb, did you find your socks?" called his mom.

"Kellie, wait. I didn't brush your hair," called her mom.

"Where are my keys?" asked Pop.

"Mimi, I think you forgot something," grinned Shannon.

Mimi stopped. She looked down and realized that she had on her furry slippers. "Don't lock the door. I've got to get my shoes," she shrieked.

"We're actually on time," sighed Pop. He and Mimi held hands as they walked into church surrounded by their children and grandchildren. "This is as good as it gets," he whispered to her. Everyone scattered to go to their Sunday school classes.

When Sunday school was over, the family sat together on the front pews of the church. The service began. After a hymn the pastor said, "This is an important day in the life of our church. One of our covenant children is ready to make her public statement of faith. She has gone through several weeks of classes, and today she presents herself to become a full member of this covenant family."

He asked Shannon to join him at the front of the church. She wore the pearls Pop had given her. "Shannon," the pastor continued, "I will ask you the questions we have studied together. These are your covenant vows before God and this congregation."

"'Do you acknowledge yourself to be a sinner in the sight of God, justly deserving His displeasure, and without hope, except through His sovereign mercy?'"*

Shannon answered, "Yes."

"'Do you believe in the Lord Jesus Christ as the Son of God and Saviour of sinners, and do you receive and trust Him alone for salvation as He is offered in the Gospel?'"*

Her eyes shone as she answered, "Yes."

"'Do you now resolve and promise, in humble reliance upon the grace of the Holy Spirit, that you endeavor to live as becometh the followers of Christ?'"*

As Shannon answered, "Yes," Mimi prayed in her heart, *Father, it's because You have kept Your promise and redeemed Shannon that she can keep this promise. Help her to continually grow in her understanding of Your love and to be compelled by Your love to live for Your glory.*

"'Do you promise to support the Church in its worship and work to the best of your ability?'"*

As Shannon answered, "Yes," Caleb thought, *This must be those responsibilities Dad mentioned. Maybe I'm not mature enough yet.*

"'Do you submit yourself to the government and discipline of the Church, and promise to strive for its purity and peace?'"*

Wow, thought Caleb as he heard Shannon answer, "Yes," *This really is bigger than I thought. I don't think I know how to strive for the purity and peace of the church.*

Then the pastor said, "Now Shannon has something else she would like to say."

Shannon smiled. At first her voice quivered just a little, but then it became strong. "I thank my Savior for His grace to me. I thank Him for giving me a Christian family, and I am grateful that they are all here with me today. I am also thankful that He has given me a covenant family. As I stand before you, I make the same covenant pledge that Ruth made hundreds of years ago: 'Where you go I will go, and where you lodge I will lodge. Your people shall be my

*Application for Membership (Norcross, GA: Presbyterian Church in America, Committee for Christian Education and Publications).

people, and your God my God. Where you die I will die, and there I will be buried. May the LORD do so to me and more also if anything but death parts me from you (Ruth 1:16-17).'"

The pastor smiled. "Shannon, in some glorious and mysterious way you are united to God's people all over the world and throughout history. Some are already in heaven, and some are yet to be born. He came and sought us to be His bride. We are His elect from every nation. Always remember that the church's foundation is Jesus Christ. He is our Lord, and His church will be victorious because He will never leave us nor forsake us."

As the congregation sang, "The Church's One Foundation," Caleb thought to himself, *Our history is* not *about dead people. This is big . . . really big.*

■

LET'S TALK

What was Shannon thankful for?

The pastor said that Shannon was united to whom?

Read the hymn "The Church's One Foundation." What does it say about the church?

The Church's One Foundation

Christ Jesus himself as the chief cornerstone. Eph. 2:20

1. The church-'s one foun - da - tion is Je - sus Christ, her Lord;
2. E - lect from ev - 'ry na - tion, yet one o'er all the earth,
3. Though with a scorn - ful won - der men see her sore op - pressed,
4. The church shall nev - er per - ish! Her dear Lord to de - fend,

she is his new cre - a - tion by wa - ter and the Word:
her char - ter of sal - va - tion one Lord, one faith, one birth;
by schis - ms rent a - sun - der, by her - e - sies dis - tressed,
to guide, sus - tain, and cher - ish, is with her to the end;

from heav'n he came and sought her to be his ho - ly bride;
one ho - ly name she bless - es, par - takes one ho - ly food,
yet saints their watch are keep - ing, their cry goes up, "How long?"
though there be those that hate her, and false sons in her pale,

with his own blood he bought her, and for her life he died.
and to one hope she press - es, with ev - 'ry grace en - dued.
And soon the night of weep - ing shall be the morn of song.
a - gainst or foe or trai - tor she ev - er shall pre - vail.

Samuel J. Stone, 1866

AURELIA 7.6.7.6.D.
Samuel S. Wesley, 1864

CHAPTER THIRTY-SIX

The Covenant, Cradle, Cross, and Crown

COVENANT PRIVILEGE AND RESPONSIBILITY: UNITY

I have given them the glory that you gave me, that they may be one as we are one: I in them and you in me. May they be brought to complete unity to let the world know that you sent me and have loved them even as you have loved me.
(John 17:22-23 NIV)

"Is everyone ready?" called Pastor Scotty. "We can't be late."

"We've got to take some pictures before we leave," insisted Heather. "The kids look so cute in the outfits Papa Sam and Mama Maggie gave them."

"I love Christmas!" exclaimed Angus as he came down the stairs holding Grace's hand.

"And I love our matching outfits," said Susie as she followed him with Joy.

Papa Sam and Mama Maggie had given Angus a plaid flannel shirt and the girls matching plaid flannel dresses. They said the outfits would be an object lesson for their story time with the children during the Christmas Eve service.

"I hope everyone knows their parts," Angus remarked as they climbed into the van. They sang Christmas carols as they drove to church.

Before Pastor Scotty preached the Christmas Eve sermon, he said, "Tonight Papa Sam and Mama Maggie are going to be grandparents for all of our covenant children. Come to the front, kids. They have a special story for you."

Papa Sam and Mama Maggie sat in rocking chairs. There was a Christmas tree beside them. The children gathered around them and sat on the floor. It was a beautiful sight.

Papa Sam began, "We need you to help us. Each time I point to you, I want you all to ask, 'Is it time?' And when Mama Maggie points to you, you're to say, 'It's time!'"

Papa Sam continued, "When and where do you think Christmas began?"

"When Jesus was born in Bethlehem," answered one of the children.

"Actually," grinned Papa Sam, "the Christmas story began *before* Jesus was born in Bethlehem. Listen carefully."

Daniel stood at the microphone. He was wearing a sport coat and tie. He looked quite spiffy. He proclaimed:

> *"Praise be to the God and Father of our Lord Jesus Christ, who has blessed us in the heavenly realms with every spiritual blessing in Christ. For he chose us in him before the creation of the world to be holy and blameless in his sight. In love he predestined us to be adopted as his sons through Jesus Christ, in accordance with his pleasure and will—to the praise of his glorious grace, which he has freely given us in the One he loves. In him we have redemption through his blood."* (Ephesians 1:3-7 NIV)

Mama Maggie continued, "The Christmas story began *before* God created the world when God the Father, Son, and Holy Spirit made a covenant, or agreement, to redeem His people. God created Adam and Eve holy and blameless, but they sinned. Sin separates us from God, but God told Adam and Eve about the covenant. He promised them that One would come who would be holy and blameless for us. God promised, 'I will be your God, you will be My people, and I will dwell among you.' But when would God keep the promise? Would Christmas be the next day . . . or the day after that? Every day Adam and Eve probably asked—"

Papa Sam pointed to the children, and they all asked, "Is it time?"

Mary stood at the microphone. "Years went by. Adam and Eve died. God kept telling His people about the promise. He told Abraham and Sarah that the Savior would come from their family. More years went by. Abraham and Sarah asked—"

Papa Sam pointed to the children. "Is it time?" they asked.

Mac had taken his place at the microphone. "God told Isaac, Jacob, Moses, and David about the promise. They asked—"

Even before Papa Sam pointed to them, the children asked, "Is it time?"

Susie was at the microphone. "God told Isaiah and Jeremiah about the promise. They asked—"

"Is it time?" came the chorus of voices.

Mama Maggie smiled. "Some people probably thought that God was not going to keep His promise. But there were some people who believed. They trusted God to do what He said He would do. One day an angel appeared to a young woman named Mary. The angel told her that she would have a baby, and His name would be Jesus, for He would save His people from their sins. The angel also told Joseph the good news. What do you think Mary and Joseph said?"

She pointed, and the children exclaimed, "It's time!"

It was Caleb's turn. He stood straight and spoke clearly. "The time had come for Jesus to be born. God became a child so that we can be His children, and His cradle was a manger."

Papa Sam spoke next. "That was not the end of Christmas. Jesus grew to be a man. He was holy and blameless, and then He gave His sinless life on the cross as the sacrifice for our sins so that we can be holy and blameless. But that's not the end of Christmas either. Jesus rose from the dead and went to His throne in heaven. He is Savior and He is King. When we repent of our sin and trust in Jesus, God covers us in the righteousness of Jesus so that we can live in His presence. He adopts us into His family."

Grace was perched on Papa Sam's knee, and Joy was snuggled in Mama Maggie's lap. Angus and

Susie stood between Papa Sam and Mama Maggie. "Do you notice anything about our grandchildren?" asked Papa Sam.

Several children responded, "They're dressed alike."

Papa Sam smiled. "When God the Father looks at us, we're all dressed exactly alike. We are dressed in the righteousness of Jesus. God doesn't love some of us more than He loves others. He loves us all with a perfect and everlasting love because we're in Christ."

Mama Maggie picked up a box with a pretty bow. She opened the lid and took out a beautiful Christmas ornament in the shape of a gift. She gave it to one of the children to hang on the tree. "Christmas is about the *covenant*. This is a covenant of grace because it is a gift that we do not deserve and cannot earn."

She reached in the box and took out another ornament in the shape of a cradle. She gave it to another child who put it on the tree. "Christmas is about the *cradle*. When Jesus was born, God kept His promise to send a Savior."

She held up an ornament shaped like a cross and gave it to another child. "Christmas is about the *cross*. Jesus died for the sins of His people."

She gave an ornament in the shape of a crown to another child. "Christmas is about the *crown*. Jesus is the King of Kings and Lord of Lords. When Jesus comes back, do you know what He will give us?"

The children listened eagerly. Cassie stood at the microphone. She said, "'When the chief Shepherd appears, you will receive the unfading crown of glory'" (1 Peter 5:4).

Papa Sam continued, "Imagine! He will give us a crown of glory. Some people don't believe the promise. Some people don't believe that Jesus came, and they don't believe that He's coming back. But God's children believe, and they ask the question—"

He pointed to the children, and they said all together, "Is it time?"

Mama Maggie smiled. "When Jesus does come back, we'll join together with all of His children who have ever lived at any time in history. There will be people from every tribe and nation. And do you know what we'll do with those crowns He gives us?"

Angus stood at the microphone. He took a deep breath. He spoke with vigor. "'[We'll] fall down before him who is seated on the throne and worship him who lives forever and ever. [We'll] cast [our] crowns before the throne, saying—'"

All of the children joined Angus to say triumphantly,

"'Worthy are you, our Lord and God,

to receive glory and honor and power,

for you created all things,

and by your will they existed and were created.'" (Revelation 4:10-11)

— ■ —

LET'S TALK

When did Christmas begin?

What are the four words that begin with c that help us understand the meaning of Christmas?

When God the Father looks at His children, how are we dressed?

What will we do with our crowns when Jesus comes back?

I will establish my covenant between me and you and your offspring after you throughout their generations for an everlasting covenant, to be God to you and to your offspring after you.
(Genesis 17:7)

I will take you to be my people, and I will be your God. . . .
(Exodus 6:7)

I will make my dwelling among you. . . . And I will walk among you and will be your God, and you shall be my people. (Leviticus 26:11-12)

I will give them a heart to know that I am the Lord, and they shall be my people and I will be their God, for they shall return to me with their whole heart.
(Jeremiah 24:7)

But this is the covenant that I will make with the house of Israel after those days, declares the Lord: I will put my law within them, and I will write it on their hearts. And I will be their God, and they shall be my people.
(Jeremiah 31:33 and Hebrews 8:10)

Behold, the virgin shall conceive and bear a son, and they shall call his name Immanuel (which means, God with us). (Matthew 1:23)

And the Word became flesh and dwelt among us, and we have seen his glory, glory as of the only Son from the Father, full of grace and truth. (John 1:14)

For we are the temple of the living God; as God said, "I will make my dwelling among them and walk among them, and I will be their God, and they shall be my people." (2 Corinthians 6:16)

Then I saw a new heaven and a new earth, for the first heaven and the first earth had passed away, and the sea was no more. And I saw the holy city, new Jerusalem, coming down out of heaven from God, prepared as a bride adorned for her husband. And I heard a loud voice from the throne saying, "Behold the dwelling place of God is with man. He will dwell with them, and they will be his people, and God himself will be with them as their God."
(Revelation 21:1-3)